THE CHILDREN'S SAFETY EDUCATION
RANGE OF SAFETY P

The products we provide are developed and produced by Kids Safetynet Ltd. They encourage children to learn important life saving messages, through the use of fictional characters where appropriate. Additional resources include lesson plans, games, puzzles and interactive media.

All of our resources have been designed and developed using an educational technique based on the 'educate, explore and enable' model.

Resources for 5-7 year olds

SELF ESTEEM - WILL POWER'S EARLY YEARS BOOK OF CHOICES

Growing up is all about making decisions and these days key life decisions are faced by younger and younger children. The 'Will Power' Early Years Book of Choices enables young people to explore issues surrounding safety, choice and rules. Topics are approached in a simple, no-nonsense manner so that young readers can use the publication as a basis of discussion in the classroom or at home with parents. Using the **'Educate, explore and enable'** model, children are encouraged to explore curriculum topics such as **'health education'** and **'substance use and misuse'**.

- **Curriculum links:** Science. Sc2 2c.that taking exercise and eating the right types and amounts of food help humans keep healthy. P.S.H.E. and Citizenship. 3a.What makes a healthy lifestyle.
  (Scotland... English, Mathematics, Science, Religious and Moral Education.)

FIRE SAFETY - DEEDEE AND DENNIS THE DRAGON

Building on the success of our Red Alert publication which features Dennis the Dragon, this charming book introduces Dennis's inquisitive younger sister Deedee. Central safety issues are dealt with in a sensitive manner so that they will stay with the children as they move through their early school years. The publication includes a mixture of stories and classroom activities, encouraging the children to **identify dangers and discover solutions**. This interactive approach to problem-solving will enable teachers to build a firm, fire safe foundation in the minds of all 5-7 year olds.

- **Curriculum links:** English En3. put their ideas in sentences, use a clear structure to organise their writing, vary their writing to suit the purpose and the reader... P.S.H.E. and Citizenship.3g. rules for and ways of keeping safe..and about people who can help them to keep safe.
  (Scotland.. English, ICT, Personal and Social Development.)

FIRST AID - EARLY YEARS FIRST AID HANDBOOK

Designed by a Paramedic for children aged 5-7 years. This colourful handbook provides a key introduction to First Aid which is both educational and entertaining. It sensitively allows young children to explore issues surrounding first aid.
Topics include: The Body; Organs; Senses and First Aid.

- **Curriculum links:** Science Sc2. 2g ... about the senses that enable humans and other animals to be aware of the world around them. P.S.H.E. and Citizenship. 3a .... what makes a healthy lifestyle
  (Scotland ... English, Personal and Social Development, Health Education.)

OUR RESOURCES

Resources for 7-11 year olds

CITIZENSHIP - JUNIOR CITIZEN HANDBOOK

Junior Citizen addresses a number of key topics that include: **Road Safety, Stranger Danger, Drugs, Alcohol, Smoking, First Aid, Hate Crime, Electricity and Gas Safety**. Designed to reinforce the serious messages taught at multi-agency child safety events each year the Junior Citizen has become a useful classroom aid for the delivery of effective P.S.H.E. in schools.

- **Curriculum links:** Art and design **1a.** record from experience and imagination, to select and record from first-hand observation and to explore ideas for different purposes. P.S.H.E. and Citizenship... **3f.** that pressure to behave in an unacceptable or risky way can come from a variety of sources, including people they know and how to ask for help and use basic techniques for resisting pressure to do wrong.
  (Scotland... Mathematics, Art and design, Personal and Social Development.)

DRUGS EDUCATION - WILL POWER'S BEWARE

Addressing elements of a child's personal and social education. Will Power presents key facts in a user-friendly fashion by inviting readers to discover more through a range of activities.
Topics covered include: Smoking, Alcohol, Drugs, My Body, Taking Control and Bullying.

- **Curriculum links:** History. **4b.** to ask and answer questions, to select and record information relevant to the focus of their enquiry. P.S.H.E. and Citizenship **4d.** to realise the nature and consequences of racism, teasing, bullying and aggressive behaviours, and how to respond to them and ask for help.
  (Scotland.... Mathematics, Science, Personal and Social Development.)

ACCIDENT PREVENTION - PLAY SAFE, STAY SAFE, KEEP SAFE

Key topics covered include **safety at home, electricity, water, beaches, building sites, roads, health and fitness, first aid, bullying and drugs**.
The handbook is specially designed to involve parents, teachers and children in projects, activities and coursework, so it entertains whilst it educates.

- **Curriculum links:** Design and technology. **3d.** communicate design ideas in different ways as they develop, bearing in mind aesthetic qualities, and the uses and purposes for which the product is intended. P.S.H.E. and Citizenship. **5d.** make real choices and decisions (for example about issues affecting their health and well-being such as smoking).
  (Scotland... Science, Personal and Social Development, Health Education.)

FIRE SAFETY - RED ALERT

Providing a comprehensive introduction to all aspects of fire safety. Covering everything from the **scientific explanation of fire, to fire prevention, the role of fire in celebration and even a fascinating journey back in time**. Red Alert has been recommended by the **National Community Fire Safety Centre**.

- **Curriculum links:** Mathematics. **4a.** to recognise the need for standard units of length, mass and capacity **4d.** use units of time and know the relationship between them. P.S.H.E. and Citizenship. **4a.** that their actions affect themselves and others.
  (Scotland... English, Personal and Social Development, Religious and Moral Education.)

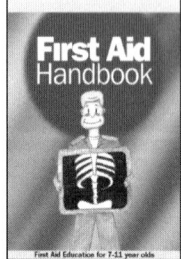

THE FIRST AID HANDBOOK

The First Aid Handbook has been written and illustrated by a qualified Paramedic for children aged 7-11 years. Topics covered include **cuts and bruises, burns, fractures, sprains, resuscitation and emergency action**.

- **Curriculum links:** Science Sc2. **2c.** that the heart acts as a pump to circulate the blood around the body. P.S.H.E. and Citizenship. **3a.** what makes a healthy lifestyle including the benefits of exercise and healthy eating **3g.** school rules about health and safety, basic emergency aid procedures and where to get help.
  (Scotland.. Science, ICT, Personal and Social Development, Health Education.)

OUR RESOURCES

OUT AND ABOUT

Out and About provides a comprehensive look at a range of primary P.S.H.E. and Citizenship issues. Young people are encouraged to **travel safely** on **foot**, **road**, **rail**, **canal** and **plane**. The activities are designed so that they not only stimulate discussion but also link closely to the child's own experiences.

- **Curriculum links:** History **11.** a study of changes in work and transport on the lives of men, women and children from different sections of society (Victorian). Science **1b.** pupils should be taught to construct simple circuits, incorporating a battery or power supply. P.S.H.E. and Citizenship... **3e.** to recognise the different risks in different situations and then decide how to behave responsibly, including sensible road use.

THE YOUNG PERSON'S GUIDE TO BULLYING

The Young Person's Guide to Bullying is an important addition to the P.S.H.E. and Citizenship range. Providing comprehensive coverage of this high-profile subject, exercises are provided that focus on victims and bullies themselves. The resource progresses naturally through to the children's own experiences and encourages them to help themselves within their school environment.

- **Curriculum links:** English **En1. 3a.** make contributions relevant to a topic and take turns in discussion. **En3. 6a.** be taught how written standard English varies in degrees of formality (e.g. letter to friend and newspaper report) P.S.H.E. and Citizenship. **4d.** taught to realise the nature and consequences of racism, teasing bullying and aggressive behaviours, and how to respond to them and ask for help.

Resources for 11-14 year olds

CITIZENSHIP - RESPECT

Exploring many of the major issues encountered by 11-14 year olds in their everyday lives. **Respect** uses real life situations to examine various citizenship issues and offers a range of useful contacts for further investigation. Topics discussed include **peer pressure, crime prevention, alcohol, drugs and solvent misuse, car crime, bullying, theft, racial harassment, personal safety, trespass and vandalism**.

- **Curriculum links:** Science **2g.** about the effects on the human body of tobacco, alcohol and other drugs and how these relate to their personal health. P.S.H.E. and Citizenship **4f.** that differences and similarities between people arise from a number of factors, including cultural, ethical, racial and religious diversity, gender and disability.
(Scotland... Personal and Social Development, Health Education, Religious and Moral Education.)

For teachers, parents and carers

A LITTLE RAY OF HOPE

We've all suffered in one way or another as a result of crime, but when a child becomes a crime victim, the effect can be more intense. Compiled with the help of police and social service child protection experts, this publication looks at the ways in which different crimes affect any child.

- **Curriculum links:** This publication is suitable for parents of child victims and as a teacher resource.

OUR RESOURCES

NATIONAL CURRICULUM REFERENCES

CURRICULUM SUBJECT	ROAD SAFETY	FIRE SAFETY	PERSONAL & COMMUNITY SAFETY	BULLYING	HATE CRIME	HEALTH EDUCATION	FIRST AID	CITIZENSHIP & COMMUNITY RESPONSIBILITY	YOUNG PEOPLE & THE LAW
ENGLISH	En1-3	En1-3	En1-3	En1-3	En1-3	En1-3	En1-3	En1-3	En1-3
MATHEMATICS	Ma4	Ma3, Ma4,1a-h, Ma4,2a-f	Ma4,2f	Ma4	Ma3, Ma4	Ma3,4a Ma4,2b	Ma3,4a	Ma3,4a	Ma4
SCIENCE	Sc3, Sc4	Sc3,2g Sc4,1a-c	Sc2,2cd		Sc3 Sc4,3c	Sc2,3a-d Sc2,g-h	Sc2,3a-h Sc3,2c	Sc2,1c	
DESIGN & TECHNOLOGY	DT1	DT1a-d 3c	DT1a		DT1a-d		DT1a-d 3c	DT1a-d	DT1a-d
ICT	1a,b	1a-c			1a-c	3a-b,5b	5b	1a-c	5a-c
HISTORY	H11a	H11a	H7,11a		H11a	H4a-b	H11a	H4a-b	H4a-b,5
GEOGRAPHY	G3f	G2,a-g	G1,a-c		G1,d-e G2,e-f, G3f		G1,a-c G3,a,d, 4a	G2a-g 3f	G2a-g
ART & DESIGN	A&D1a-c	1a-c				1a-c	1a-c	1a-c	1a-c
MUSIC	M,3b	M1a-c	M2a-b	M2a-b		M3b		M2a-b	M5a-e
PE	7c							7c	
P.S.H.E. / CITIZENSHIP (non statutory)	1a-c 3e	2d	2b	1a-f 2bc 4d-g	1a-b 1d-g 2b,c,j,k, 4a	3a-d 3e	3a-b 3g	2a,c,h,i 4a,b,f,g	2g,h,j,k

OUR RESOURCES

CURRICULUM CODINGS FOR ENGLAND AND WALES

PUBLICATION TITLE	ENGLISH	MATHEMATICS	SCIENCE	DESIGN & TECHNOLOGY	ICT	HISTORY	GEOGRAPHY	ART & DESIGN	MUSIC	PE	P.S.H.E. CITIZENSHIP	RE
5 - 7 YEARS												
WILL POWER'S EARLY YEARS BOOK OF CHOICES	En1-3	Ma3	Sc2 2c	1a-e				1a-b			1a-e 3a-e	
DEEDEE & DENNIS THE DRAGON	En1-3	Ma3	Sc3,2b Sc4, 3a		1a-c			1a-b			2d, 2g 4a	
EARLY YEARS FIRST AID HANDBOOK	En1-3	Ma3 Ma4	Sc2 2a,c,d,g	1a-e				1a-b			3a-g	
7 - 11 YEARS												
WILL POWER'S BEWARE	En1-3	Ma4	Sc2,3 2a,c,d	1a-d		2c-d 4a-b 5a-c		1a-c			3a-g, 4d, 5d	
RED ALERT	En1-3	Ma2 Ma3, 4	Sc3 2g, 1bc		1a-c	1a-b 2a-d	5a-b	1a-c 2a-c	2a-b 5e		4a 4b	✓
FIRST AID HANDBOOK	En1-3	Ma3 Ma4	Sc2 a-h		1a-c	1a-b 4a		1a-c			3a-g	
JUNIOR CITIZEN HANDBOOK	En1-3	Ma3 Ma4	Sc2a-h Sc3, 2g	2a-d 3a-c	1a-c			1a-c			1a-c, 2c 4a-g, 3f	
PLAY SAFE, STAY SAFE, KEEP SAFE	En1-3	Ma4	Sc2,Sc1 Sc4, 3bc	2a-d 3a-c		5a-c		1a-c			1b, 3a-g 4d, 5d	
BULLYING	En1-3	Ma4									1a-f, 2bc 4d-g	✓
TRANSPORT SAFETY	En1-3	Ma4	Sc1	1a-d	1a-c 2a			1a-c			3e,3g 4a	
11 - 14 YEARS												
RESPECT YOUR LIFE, YOUR CHOICE	En1-3	Ma3 Ma4	2b 2g,h	1a-d				1a-c			1a-d, 2a-d 2h,i, 3f,g 4a-g, 5a-i	✓
A LITTLE RAY OF HOPE					THIS PUBLICATION IS SUITABLE FOR PARENTS OF CHILD VICTIMS AND TEACHERS.							

OUR RESOURCES

CURRICULUM CODINGS FOR SCOTLAND

PUBLICATION TITLE	LEVELS	ASPECTS OF LEARNING / SUBJECTS
WILL POWER'S EARLY YEARS BOOK OF CHOICES	A-C	English, Mathematics, Science, Technology, Art and Design, Personal and Social Development, Health Education, Religious and Moral Education.
DEEDEE AND DENNIS THE DRAGON	A-C	English, Mathematics, Science, ICT, Art and Design, Personal and Social Development.
EARLY YEARS FIRST AID HANDBOOK	A-C	English, Mathematics, Science, Technology, Art and Design, Personal and Social Development, Health Education.
WILL POWER'S BEWARE	B-E	English, Mathematics, Science, Technology, Art and Design, Personal and Social Development.
RED ALERT	B-E	English, Mathematics, Science, ICT, Social Subjects, Art and Design, Music, Personal and Social Development, Religious and Moral Education.
FIRST AID HANDBOOK	B-E	English, Mathematics, Science, Technology, ICT, Social Subjects, Art and Design, Health Education, Personal and Social Development.
JUNIOR CITIZEN HANDBOOK	B-E	English, Mathematics, Science, Technology, ICT, Art and Design, Personal and Social Development.
PLAY SAFE, STAY SAFE, KEEP SAFE	B-E	English, Mathematics, Science, Technology, ICT, Art and Design, Personal and Social Development, Health Education.
BULLYING	B-E	English, Mathematics, Personal and Social Development, Religious and Moral Education.
OUT AND ABOUT	B-E	English, Mathematics, Science, Technology, ICT, Art and Design, Personal and Social Development.
RESPECT YOUR LIFE, YOUR CHOICE	B-E	English, Mathematics, Science, Technology, ICT, Art and Design, Personal and Social Development, Religious and Moral Education, Health Education.

OUR RESOURCES

SCOTTISH LINKS

	ROAD SAFETY	FIRE SAFETY	PERSONAL & COMMUNITY SAFETY	BULLYING	HATE CRIME	HEALTH EDUCATION	FIRST AID	CITIZENSHIP & COMMUNITY RESPONSIBILITY	YOUNG PEOPLE & THE LAW
LANGUAGE	✓	✓	✓	✓	✓	✓	✓	✓	✓
MATHEMATICS	✓	✓	✓	✓	✓	✓	✓	✓	✓
ENVIRONMENTAL STUDIES, SOCIETY SCIENCE TECHNOLOGY	✓	✓	✓		✓	✓	✓	✓	✓
EXPRESSIVE ARTS PHYSICAL EDUCATION	✓	✓	✓	✓	✓	✓	✓	✓	✓
RELIGIOUS AND MORAL EDUCATION	✓	✓	✓	✓	✓	✓	✓	✓	✓

OUR RESOURCES

CONTENTS

RESOURCES 1-6

NATIONAL CURRICULUM REFERENCES 4-7

ROAD SAFETY

Be Seen - What Can You Do 11
Vision Zero 12
On Your Bike 13
Watch Out - Crossing The Road 14
Safe Onboard
- Seat Belts - Cycle Helmets 15
Motorway Safety 16
Key Links Chart 17

FIRE SAFETY

What To Do In An Emergency 19
Home Safety - Smoke Alarms 20
Firework Safety 21
Electrical Fires 22
Hoaxes 23
Fire Prevention 24
Key Links Chart 25

PERSONAL AND COMMUNITY SAFETY

Strangers 27
Accidents At Home 28
Rail Safety 29
Countryside and Farm Safety 30

Water Safety 31
Safety On The Streets 32
Key Links Chart 33

BULLYING

How Does It Work? 35
Causes Of Bullying 36
Being Assertive............................. 37
Confronting Bullying 38
Beating the Bullies 39
A Survey On Bullying 40
Key Links Chart 41

HATE CRIME

Legal Rights 43
My Rights.................................... 44
Racism And Sexism 45
P.L.A.N. 46
Hate Crime 47
What Are We Going To Do? 48
Key Links Chart 49

HEALTH EDUCATION

Smoking - The Facts....................... 51
Saying No To Smoking 52
Alcohol - The Facts........................ 53
The Dangers Of Alcohol................... 54
Drugs That Help 55
Drug Abuse 56
Key Links Chart 57

CONTENTS

FIRST AID

What To Do In An Emergency	59
Saving Lives	60
Recovery Facts	61
Shock And Treatment	62
A Basic First Aid Kit	63
Simple First Aid	64
Key Links Chart	65

CITIZENSHIP AND COMMUNITY RESPONSIBILITIES

Safety In Numbers	67
Friendship	68
Similarities And Differences	69
Making Decisions	70
Part of The Community	71
Community Groups	72
Key Links Chart	73

THE LAW AND YOUNG PEOPLE

What Is The Law?	75
Saying No	76
Car Crime	77
Alcohol, Drugs, Solvent Abuse And The Law	78
Trespass And Vandalism	79
Shoplifting And Other Forms Of Theft	80
Key Links Chart	81

USEFUL CONTACTS 82

KEY

- **A** - Art and Design
- **DT** - Design and Technology
- **E** - English
- **G** - Geography
- **H** - History
- **ICT** - Information and Communication Technology
- **M** - Mathematics
- **Ms** - Music
- **PE** - Physical Education
- **S** - Science

Some activities are suitable for development at 5 - 7 years at teachers discretion.

NOTE:

Curriculum links are examples. Many more can be found when expanding study of particular areas.

ROAD SAFETY

PURPOSE:
- **To provide young people with knowledge and understanding of road safety in their own locality.**
- **To build up a wider knowledge of road safety outside their own area of experience**
- **To encourage individual thinking and decision making**

FACT: Almost half the children who get hurt on our roads are on foot.

FACT: Most children injured are boys.

Page 11	**BE SEEN** **WHAT CAN YOU DO**
Page 12	**VISION ZERO**
Page 13	**ON YOUR BIKE**
Page 14	**WATCH OUT** **CROSSING THE ROAD**
Page 15	**SAFE ONBOARD** **SEAT BELTS** **CYCLE HELMETS**
Page 16	**MOTORWAY SAFETY**
Page 17	**KEY LINKS CHART**

TEACHER'S NOTE:
RESOURCES FOR ROAD SAFETY INCLUDE:
- Play Safe, Stay Safe, Keep Safe (7-11 years)
- Junior Citizen Handbook (7-11 years)
- Out and About (7-11 years)

ROAD SAFETY

BE SEEN

PURPOSE: To investigate fluorescent materials and the need to be seen.

TEACHER INFORMATION:
It is important that as a pedestrian you can be seen. Light colours and special fluorescent colours stand out during the day and at night. Some materials are obviously better at reflecting light.

In bad weather pedestrians may not be easily seen and care should be taken to wear something bright or fluorescent. At night adults and young people should wear something white or reflective so that drivers can see them.

It is a good idea for children to choose a safe route to school, one that avoids hazards and other dangerous places. It needs to be well lit and children should avoid isolated places.

KEY ACTIVITY (S):
YOU WILL NEED: torch, card, flat mirror, bendy mirror, glossy surface, matt surface, reflective surface, different materials e.g. matt, fluorescent, shiny, reflective.

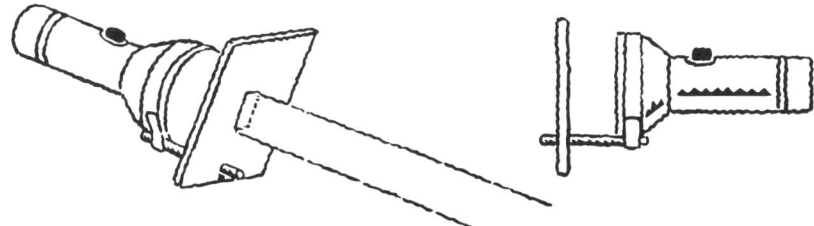

Cut a small hole in the piece of card. Fix it to the front of the torch. Shine the narrow beam of light onto each of the surfaces from different angles. Record your results. Was the reflected light easily seen? Which surface was the most reflective and why? Now try out some shiny, reflective, matt and fluorescent materials. Which material shows up the best in daylight, in a dark place, and by torchlight?

MATERIAL	DAYLIGHT	DARK PLACE	TORCHLIGHT
SHINY			
MATT			
REFLECTIVE			
FLUORESCENT			

FURTHER IDEAS:
- Work out a variety of safe routes from home to school. (M)
- Work out how many times the children cross the road from home to school. Is there a safer route? (M)
- Who crosses the road the most times in the class? (M)
- Write a story about a journey on foot to a new school. (E)
- Carry out research into the origination of cat's eyes. How do they work? (H)
- Design a poster entitled, 'Being Seen'. (DT)
- Make up a play about a journey from home to school. (E)
- Write a letter to the local road safety officer inviting them to come in and talk to the class. (E)
- Work out some different ways in which road signs could be recognised e.g. shape, size and colour. (M,DT)
- Take a look at the Highway Code and the section on pedestrians.
- Invite one of the emergency services into school and look at their reflective clothing and the way they mark their vehicles so that they can be seen clearly during the day and at night. (E,DT,S)

ROAD SAFETY

VISION ZERO

PURPOSE: To investigate ways of improving safety on our roads.

TEACHER INFORMATION:

It is important that children are aware of measures that are taking place in this country and abroad to help improve safety on the road.

Vision Zero, a policy adopted by the Swedish Government four years ago, stated that their ultimate aim was that no-one would be killed or injured on any Swedish road. An impossible task but an ideal to aim for. One of their main worries was the speed of vehicles. In ten years it is hoped that the number of accidents will be reduced from a third to a quarter.

As part of Vision Zero safety measures the Swedish Government looked at:

- Central crash barriers.
- Roundabouts.
- Speed limits.
- Special speed zones in urban areas. e.g. near schools and play areas.
- Making road users aware that they are responsible for their own safety and that of others.
- Wider use of bicycle helmets.
- Not driving under the influence of alcohol or drugs.
- Compulsory use of winter tyres.
- Safer motorways.
- Speed cameras people know about.

Research is presently going on in Sweden to produce a series of locks which would prevent drivers over the limit from starting or even entering their vehicles.

New roads and newly designed vehicles are a way forward. Roads designed to include all weather and night lighting together with better means of evacuation from your vehicle i.e. emergency exit doors, improved braking and anti locking devices.

KEY ACTIVITY (DT)

YOU WILL NEED: toy car, pens, glue, paint, board, paper.

- Design a road layout which includes traffic calming devices and speed zones. Include on your model sleeping policemen, special speed barriers and speed limit signs.

FURTHER IDEAS:

- Carry out a traffic survey on the number of vehicles passing by the school. Carry out the survey in the morning, at lunchtime and in the afternoon. When is the quietest and busiest time of the day? How could the speed of vehicles be reduced outside the school? (M)
- Get the children to write to a local councillor with suggestions for improving road safety in your area. (E)
- Design a safe car. Incorporate a range of safety features into the design. (DT)
- Surf the Internet for information on traffic schemes in the following cities:- Bath (UK), Los Angeles (USA), Sydney (Australia), Athens (Greece). (ICT)

ON YOUR BIKE

PURPOSE: To discuss why it is important to have a safe bike and understanding the basic rules of cycling.

TEACHER INFORMATION:
Cycling is a cheap form of transport and environmentally very friendly.

Riding a bicycle is a healthy way of keeping fit and children should be encouraged to realise the benefits. However cyclists are at risk when they go out on their bicycles and it is very easy for motorists not to see them. Children therefore, need to know the basic rules of the road and how best to be visible and easy to spot.
It is important that bikes are the right size for the rider and that they are safe to ride. They should have proper lights and red reflectors at the rear.

Over 8 out of 10 cyclists who have an accident suffer head injuries, so it is important to wear a snug fitting cycle helmet.

It is vital that cyclists can be seen so they should wear bright clothing during the day and reflective armbands or belts at night.

If possible they should stick to cycle routes or special cycle tracks.

At Toucan crossings cyclists and pedestrians are allowed to cross at the same time however, on other crossings cyclists should get off and push their bikes to the other side.

You should always use a cycle lock when you leave your bike and remember that you shouldn't cycle on the pavement unless there is a cycle sign on display.

SAMPLE CYCLING RULES:
- When riding along a narrow road you should ride in single file.
- Always keep both hands on the handlebars when riding and feet firmly on the pedals.
- Always look around when moving off.
- Be careful of parked cars, people crossing the road and cars manoeuvring.

KEY ACTIVITY (E):
YOU WILL NEED: pencil, crayons, paper.

Draw a large bicycle on a piece of paper. Make a set of labels for the different parts of the bike explaining the different safety features and things to remember when out cycling.

It is important to have a bell fitted to the bike.

FURTHER IDEAS:
- Make up a set of cycle rules. (E)
- Design a safe bicycle. (DT)
- Conduct a survey of people in the class who have bicycles. (M)
- Find out how a battery light works. (S)
- Investigate the material used for making cycle helmets. (S)
- Draw a map of your area and highlight in any cycle routes. (G)
- Find out more about countries where bicycles are very popular e.g. Holland and China. (G, ICT)
- Write a story or play about an adventure on a bicycle. (E)

WATCH OUT

PURPOSE: To explain the importance of the Green Cross Code and pedestrian safety.

TEACHER INFORMATION:

50% of people injured every year are children. Most children between 8 and 11, hurt on our roads are boys. It is therefore very important that children understand that footpaths can be dangerous places. If there is a footpath they should use it and always keep as far away from the traffic as possible. If there isn't a footpath they should walk on the right side facing oncoming traffic and keep as close as possible to the edge. They need to be careful near bends and always walk in single file. It is always a good idea to wear bright clothing or something reflective. Always use the Green Cross Code.

THE GREEN CROSS CODE:

1. Find the safest place to cross, then stop.
2. Stand on the pavement near the kerb.
3. Look all around for traffic and listen.
4. If traffic is coming let it pass.
5. When there isn't any traffic near walk straight across the road.
6. Keep looking and listening for traffic while you cross.

Remember: THINK FIRST - STOP - USE YOUR EYES AND EARS - WAIT UNTIL IT IS SAFE TO CROSS - LOOK AND LISTEN - ARRIVE ALIVE

Crossings are much safer places to cross. There are six main ones:
- **Subways and footbridges**. These are fine for crossing over or under roads.
- **School patrols**. These are usually outside school and are one way of safely crossing the road.
- **Traffic Islands**. These should be used in two stages. They are often in the centre of roads.
- **Toucans and Puffins Crossings**. Puffins are for foot pedestrians and Toucans for both cyclists and pedestrians.
- **Zebra Crossings**. Zebras have beacons at both ends. Children need to be told they should stop on the pavement and wait until the traffic has passed before crossing on the stripes. They should always look and listen as they cross.
- **Pelicans**. These work by pressing a button when the red man appears. When the green man appears make sure that the traffic has stopped before crossing. If the green man is flashing do not cross. However if you are already crossing there will be time for you to get to the other side.

TAKE CARE:

- In bad weather • Crossing between parked cars • In car parks • At night
  It is dangerous to use skateboards and roller blades on the roads.

KEY ACTIVITY (A):

YOU WILL NEED: paints, crayons, paper.
Draw and paint a poster on the Green Cross Code. Make it bright, easy to understand and large enough to see.

FURTHER IDEAS:

- Write out the instructions for using **a.** Zebra Crossing, **b.** Pelican Crossing, **c.** School Patrol. Write the instructions **a.** For younger children and **b.** As part of a letter. (E)
- Conduct a survey to find out how many times children in the class cross the road on their way to and from school. (M)
- Make up a rhyme or song on how to cross the road safely. (Ms)
- Investigate the dangers of walking to school one hundred and fifty years ago. How have the roads improved? What will it be like walking to school in one hundred years time. (E,H)
- See what you can find out on the Internet about deaths and injuries from road traffic accidents in this country and abroad. Make contact with a school in another country and find out about their journeys from home to school and back. (ICT)
- Play a traffic light game - red to stop and green to go. Everyone must stop when red is called out. The last one to stop is out. Green means go. Who is the last person left? (PE)
- Find out the stopping distances at different speeds. Produce a chart or graph to show the different distances. (M)

ROAD SAFETY

SAFE ONBOARD

PURPOSE: To discuss the importance of wearing a cycle helmet and seat belts.

TEACHER INFORMATION:

90% of cyclists who have accidents suffer head injuries. It is therefore very important to wear a cycle helmet. Make sure that it fits properly and you have it the right way round!

When riding in a car always wear the seatbelt. With over 500 million cars in the world there are bound to be accidents!

Not wearing a seatbelt means that you are breaking the law. Always make sure that you wear the seat belt. Some cars are also fitted with special child belts or child seats (especially for younger children). These can include booster cushions. In a crash at 30mph you will be thrown forward with the same force as an elephant.

Once you have closed the door make sure that you do not lean out of the window, throw things or distract the driver.

You must also stay seated so that the driver can see out of the back window.

KEY ACTIVITY (DT,A,E)

YOU WILL NEED: paints, crayons, pencil, paper, card.

Prepare a series of leaflets on the importance of wearing seat belts or encouraging people to consider using alternatives to their car. This could be based around reducing the number of cars outside the school gates in the mornings and afternoons. The children could think about car sharing schemes, walking to school in a group, taking the bus or train.

This idea could be expanded further to include an assembly on the subject and also a series of posters.

FURTHER IDEAS:

- Have a discussion on why seat belts are so important. (E)
- Paint some posters on the theme of reducing speed limits. (A)
- Investigate different ways of reducing the speed of cars in built up areas. e.g. sleeping policemen. (E)
- Test out a variety of seat belt designs using a toy car or skateboard and a ramp. Put a doll onto the skateboard and let it go down the slope. What happens when it hits the floor? Now try the same experiment but tie the doll to the skateboard with some form of belt. What happens now? (S)
- Design a new type of safe cycle helmet. (DT)
- Carry out a survey of the different speed limits in your area. (G)
- Write a story about a journey you have made or would like to make. (E)
- Write to several car manufacturers and ask what kind of safety measures they have included in their latest range of cars. (E)
- See what you can find out on the Internet about the use of seat belts in other countries. (ICT)

MOTORWAY SAFETY

PURPOSE: To look at safety on motorways.

TEACHER INFORMATION:
- The speed limit on UK motorways is 70 mph.
- You can only stop on the hard shoulder in an emergency. You can make a call for help from the emergency call boxes which are linked to police motorway control.
- You are not allowed to make U turns.
- You are not allowed on motorway embankments.
- You should never attempt to cross a motorway.

In this country over 20 million people have their own vehicles. Today motorways are one of the most important ways of getting around. They are both fast and wide. When driving on a motorway there are certain rules that you must obey.

Motorways are often built around towns and villages. They can cost a great deal of money and have a great effect on communities. If people do not agree with the planned route they may protest. Sometimes this involves meetings with planners, councillors and protesters. Some protesters take to the trees whilst others have been known to illegally block existing roads to make their point.

KEY ACTIVITY(E)
YOU WILL NEED: paper, crayons, pencils, pens, rulers, large sheets of paper.

The council has decided to build a motorway link road which will pass very close to your village. The road will cut across fields, go through a wood which contains rare plants and destroy a number of badger setts. There is also a castle in the village.

Do you think the motorway should be built? Get the children to compose an imaginary letter to the council stating why they think it is a bad or good idea.

Divide the class into two and get one side to take the role of the planners and one the protesters. Hold a debate in which the two sides come face to face. Instruct the planners to make plans showing where the road will go.

Get the other side to produce a leaflet protesting against the road putting forward their point of view.

Each side should then put their views forward at an assembly. Ask the rest of the school to listen and then vote whether or not they think the link road should go ahead.

FURTHER IDEAS:
- Discuss what is wrong with these activities:
    - walking your dog along the emergency lane of the motorway.
    - playing football on the embankment.
    - stopping the car on the motorway and having a picnic.
    - travelling at 95mph along the motorway.
    - walking across the motorway. (E)
- Construct a model showing a cross section of motorway or a motorway bypass. (A,DT)
- If a car travels at 70mph for two hours, then four and half hours, then seven hours, how far will it have gone altogether? (M)
- Produce a short play on a journey and breakdown along a motorway. (E)
- Work out a route between London and Manchester using only motorways. (M)
- Draw a series of motorway signs (A). Make up a new one to show that vehicles should not make a u-turn on a motorway. (DT)

KEY LINKS

MATHEMATICS:
Be Seen
Vision Zero
On Your Bike
Watch Out
Motorway Safety

ENGLISH:
Be Seen
Vision Zero
Safe Onboard
Motorway Safety
Watch Out
On Your Bike

SCIENCE:
On Your Bike
Be Seen
Safe Onboard

HISTORY:
Be Seen
Watch Out

GEOGRAPHY:
Be Seen
On Your Bike
Onboard
Motorway Safety

DESIGN AND TECHNOLOGY:
Be Seen
Vision Zero
On Your Bike
Safe Onboard
Motorway Safety

MUSIC:
Watch Out

ART & DESIGN:
Watch Out
Safe Onboard
Motorway Safety

PE:
Watch Out

ICT:
Vision Zero
On Your Bike
Watch Out
Safe Onboard

FIRE SAFETY

PURPOSE:
- **To provide information and develop an awareness of fire safety.**
- **To build up a wider knowledge of fire safety within the children's own experience and beyond.**
- **To encourage individual thinking and decision making.**

FACT: Fire is a chemical process. The fire triangle occurs when materials that will burn mix with oxygen from the atmosphere and a source of heat.

FACT: The Great Fire of London in 1666 burned for three days and destroyed 80% of all of the City of London's buildings.

Page 19	**WHAT TO DO IN AN EMERGENCY**
Page 20	**HOME SAFETY - SMOKE ALARMS**
Page 21	**FIREWORK SAFETY**
Page 22	**ELECTRICAL FIRES**
Page 23	**HOAXES**
Page 24	**FIRE PREVENTION**
Page 25	**KEY LINKS CHART**

TEACHER'S NOTE:
RESOURCES FOR FIRE SAFETY INCLUDE:
- Deedee The Dragon (5-7 years)
- Red Alert (7-11 years)
- Play Safe, Stay Safe, Keep Safe (7-11 years)
- Junior Citizen Handbook (7-11 years)

WHAT TO DO IN AN EMERGENCY

PURPOSE: To explain how to make an emergency 999 call and what to do if fire breaks out.

TEACHER INFORMATION:
It is important that children know the correct procedure for making a 999 call. All 999 calls are free. When making a call you should remain calm.

To make a call...
- Lift the handset and dial 999.
- A voice will ask you which service you require. It will either be Police, Fire or Ambulance. You may also request the Coastguard, Cave Rescue or Mountain Rescue.
- You will be asked the number you are calling from, your name, and details about the emergency. The operator will ask where the emergency has occurred and what has happened.
- You should stay calm at all times and answer the questions clearly.

If you are in a building and trapped by fire...
- You should remain calm.
- If you can close the doors to stop the smoke getting in. Don't open a door if when you test it with the back of your hand it feels warm.
- If you can get out move as quickly as you can.
- Dial 999 if you can get to a phone.
- Block any gaps around doors to stop smoke getting in. This can be done with towels, blankets, or pieces of clothing.
- Don't stop to collect your things.
- If your clothes catch fire then remember to stop/drop/roll: You shouldn't move about. You should drop onto the floor. You should roll on the ground to put the flames out.

KEY ACTIVITY (DT):
YOU WILL NEED: pencil, crayons, card, paper.

Imagine that you are one of the designers for the fire service.
- Design a new uniform to be worn by both male and female fire-fighters. See if you can incorporate some special features on the uniform for fighting fires.
- Design a new type of fire engine that can fight fires on land and in water. When you have finished your design you could build a model of it.

FURTHER IDEAS:
- Make up a fire fighting board game with your own set of rules. (M,E,A)
- Write a report for your local paper on a fire either at your home or in the park. (E)
- Invite a fire-fighter into school to talk about how the fire service responds to 999 calls. (E)
- Test out some different materials and see which of them burns the easiest. (S)
- Investigate how the fire service started. (H)
- How do they control and put out bush fires in Australia and forest fires in the USA and Canada? (G)
- Search the Web and see what you can find out about fire services abroad. (ICT)
- Make up a play about using the 999 service. (E)

FIRE SAFETY

HOME SAFETY - SMOKE ALARMS

PURPOSE: To find out how best to protect your home and the use of smoke alarms.

TEACHER INFORMATION:

There are over 34,000 fire fighters in England and Wales and 4,500 in Scotland. There are also volunteer fire crews dotted around the country in rural areas.

Every year the fire services are called out to around 850,000 fires (this figure includes false alarms), around 800 people die and 13,000 are injured because of fire related incidents.

The first real fire prevention was started by William the Conqueror who ordered people to put out their fires at the end of the day (sunset). They used a metal cover to do this (couvre feu) the word curfew comes from this. Before this time the Romans had their own fire watch services known as vigiles.
(Get the children to talk about other ways they think their homes are at risk from fire.)

Smoke alarms can reduce the risk of death and injury if a fire breaks out. It is important to check the batteries regularly and make sure that they are in working order.

Smoke alarms save lives by giving people a little more time to get out of the building. They should be fixed to a ceiling usually in a hall and/or on the upstairs landing. If there is any smoke then the alarm will make a high pitched sound. Some also have a high intensity light which comes on at the same time as the alarm.

80% of people killed in fires die because of the smoke.

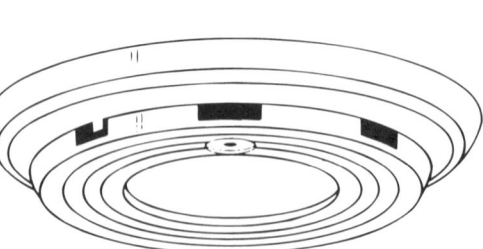

KEY ACTIVITY(DT)
YOU WILL NEED: pencil, paper.
- Carry out a school or home safety check. Go round and see if you can spot any dangers that might help or start a fire.
- Write down a list of things that should be investigated. Carry out your survey room by room. When you have finished, draw a plan showing where the main hazards are. e.g. At school lots of litter piled up. At home, a frayed wire, overloaded electrical sockets etc.
- Produce a booklet entitled 'At Risk' which explains about the fire dangers in the home or at school. Where were the greatest dangers? Who is at greatest risk in the home, at school?

FURTHER IDEAS:
- Find out how a smoke alarm works. Why has it got a test button? Why does it give off a high pitched sound when it goes off? (S)
- Find out how some famous fires of the past started e.g. Crystal Palace. (H)
- Make up a file about fire prevention. (E)
- Ask a fire prevention officer to come in and talk about good practices at school and in the home. (E)
- Carry out a survey on how many people in the school have smoke alarms in their homes. (M)
- Make a plan showing an escape route from your home and from your school. (A,DT)
- Make a drawing of your home, mark in the best places for smoke alarms. (DT)

FIREWORK SAFETY

PURPOSE: To teach the basic Firework Code and to understand what to do in an emergency.

TEACHER INFORMATION:

Fireworks were invented thousands of years ago in China and were probably first used in Britain in 1486 at the wedding of Henry VII. They are also used in a variety of religious festivals such as Diwali and during the Chinese New Year.

In recent years fireworks have not only been used on November 5th but also at New Year, for birthday celebrations and at open air concerts. Every year they cause a large number of injuries.

The temperature of a sparkler can reach 2,000 C whilst a rocket can travel up to 150mph.

Between 1994 and 1998 more than 6,000 people were injured by fireworks. Young children are most at risk from sparklers and around half of all fireworks accidents happen to under 16s.

Bonfires can also be very dangerous and get out of hand. Always stand behind safety barriers at displays and never throw anything onto the fire.

FIREWORK CODE:

- Only buy fireworks marked with BS7114
- Follow the instructions carefully
- Stand well back
- Never put fireworks in your pockets
- Never misuse fireworks
- Keep all fireworks in a closed box
- Light fireworks at arms length using the correct type of taper.
- Never return to a lit firework
- Never throw fireworks
- Keep pets indoors
- If you are lighting sparklers make sure you wear gloves and never give sparklers to children under five. Adults should light fireworks and there should always be a bucket of water on hand. Fireworks that are finished should never be thrown onto a bonfire. **NEVER FOOL WITH FIREWORKS!**

IN AN EMERGENCY:

1. Cool burns under cold water immediately.
2. Do not touch burnt skin.
3. Cover it with something clean that will not stick to the burn.
4. If someone catches light remember STOP/DROP/ROLL.
5. Get help or dial 999 in an emergency.

KEY ACTIVITY (DT,A)

YOU WILL NEED: card, crayons, paints, pencil, ruler.

Design and make a box suitable for a selection of fireworks. Then make some mock fireworks. These should include rockets, catherine wheels, sparklers etc. Make sure that they fit into your box. Include a sheet on the firework code. Decorate the outside of the box and ensure there is a safety warning.

FURTHER IDEAS:

- Write out a firework poem in the shape of a firework using lots of firework sounds. (E)
- Find out what Guy Fawkes got up to. Write an account of the events in the style of a news report or as a play (H,E).
- Investigate how fireworks are used in different festivals. If possible get a parent or local person to come in and talk about Diwali or the Chinese New Year. (E)
- Create a large painting or mural based on a firework display. (A)
- Produce a series of firework safety posters. Display them around the school. (DT,A)
- Using a search engine find out how fireworks are used abroad. (ICT)
- Make up your own firework picture or firework poem using the computer. (ICT,E)
- Construct a graph showing which are the most popular fireworks in the class. (M)
- Ask a local doctor or nurse to come in and talk about the dangers of fireworks and possible injuries caused. (E)

ELECTRICAL FIRES

PURPOSE: To explain the dangers of electrical fires.

TEACHER INFORMATION:
Faulty electrical items and wiring can cause fires. And so it is very important that you make sure that wires are properly insulated. Plugs should be correctly connected and checked. Ensure the correctly rated fuse is being used.

Some causes of electrical fires:
- Overloaded plugs
- Frayed wires
- Leaving electrical appliances unattended e.g. irons, fires.
- Leaving young children close to electrical appliances, plugs or wires
- Remember be aware of hazards.
- Electricity can be extremely dangerous in other ways and can kill or cause injury. Domestic supplies are usually set at 240 volts. This is a considerable amount of electricity.
- Never touch a socket or plug with wet hands
- Mains electricity and power from car batteries can kill.

KEY ACTIVITY (S)
YOU WILL NEED: A simple electrical circuit consisting of a 4.5 battery, torch bulb of 3 volts, three wires and several objects (see list).

Make up your circuit and test to see which of these objects conducts electricity:
- Piece of wood
- Metal spoon
- Paper clip
- String
- Copper wire
- Cork

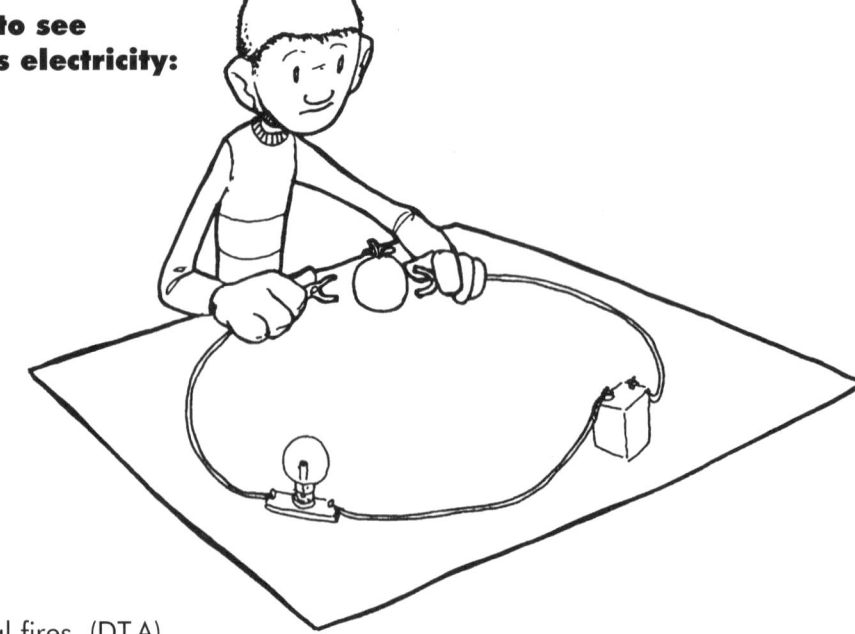

FURTHER IDEAS:
- Design a poster to explain electrical fires. (DT,A)
- Write a news report about an imaginary electrical fire. (E)
- Find out who invented the first light bulb, radio and television. (H)
- Conduct a survey of your school or home and mark on a map possible electrical danger points. (M)
- Make up an advert and jingle on the dangers of fires from electrical faults. (Ms)
- Draw a plug marking where the different coloured wires should go. (S)
- Check fuse ratings for electrical equipment e.g. iron 13 amp, radio 3 amp. (S)

FIRE SAFETY

HOAXES

PURPOSE: To explain the dangers of making a hoax call.

TEACHER INFORMATION:

Hoax calls are a major problem for the fire brigade and the other emergency services. These false calls are often made for fun with little thought of the consequences. Hoax calls tie up equipment and personnel. They often happen when youngsters are in a group and want to show off to their friends. All calls are treated as the real thing and so if a call comes in a fire engine, police car or ambulance will be sent to that address. If a real fire or accident occurs a few minutes later then it may not be possible to send a crew straight away. This could cause loss of life, injury or loss of property. **When anyone makes a false call they are putting everyone at risk.**

What is wrong with making this call? Why is it dangerous?

KEY ACTIVITY (E)

YOU WILL NEED: A group of children.

Imagine that the children are out of school in a gang. They start talking about making a hoax call as a bit of a laugh. They all think its a good idea except one child. Make up a play about what happens next.

FURTHER IDEAS:

- Invite a fire-fighter or member of the ambulance service to talk about the dangers of making hoax calls. (E)
- Discuss what kind of situations might lead to a hoax call being made. (E)
- Write a story that demonstrates how making a hoax call can be the start of a disaster. (E)
- Make a list of people who may be at risk if a hoax call is made. (E)

FIRE SAFETY

FIRE PREVENTION

PURPOSE: To examine how dangerous fires are and look at ways in which they might be prevented.

TEACHER INFORMATION:

Fire-fighters not only fight fires but also deal with accidents, chemical spillage, flooding, people who are trapped, collapsed buildings, and fire prevention. They train for about four months and then are attached to a station as a probationer for between one to two years. They become fully fledged fire-fighters after four years.

Whilst the fire service is employed to deal with fires and other problems there are various ways that we can help prevent fires from occurring.

Every year over 600 people are killed and 15,000 injured in fires started in the home.

There are lots of ways of helping to prevent fires in the home:

- Never leave cookers unattended.
- Always make sure adults put out cigarettes and pipes.
- Always check plugs and electrical items for faults.
- Beware of lighted candles.
- Be careful with open fires.
- Heaters should always be away from clothes.
- Matches and lighters should be locked away.

KEY ACTIVITY (A,DT)

YOU WILL NEED: large sheet of paper, pencil, crayons.

Draw a picture or plan of your living room or kitchen circling the most dangerous spots. You could also do this for your classroom.

FURTHER IDEAS:

- Find out how many major fires there have been in your area in the last year? How many of these were started deliberately? Produce a graph showing which types of properties have suffered the most. (M)
- Make a leaflet on fire prevention in school or homes. (A,DT)
- Arrange for the school to carry out a fire drill. Invite the fire brigade to be present to see how well it was done. (E)
- Write a letter to your local supermarket asking what they have done to prevent fires from breaking out and what measures are in place if a fire should occur. (E)
- Sing London's Burning, and then put new words to it, linked to fire prevention. (Ms)

FIRE SAFETY

KEY LINKS

MATHEMATICS: Emergency
Home Safety
Firework Safety
Electrical Fires
Fire Prevention

ENGLISH: Emergency
Home Safety
Firework Safety
Hoaxes
Fire Prevention

SCIENCE: Emergency
Home Safety
Electrical Fires

HISTORY: Emergency
Home Safety
Electrical Fires

GEOGRAPHY: Emergency

DESIGN AND TECHNOLOGY: Emergency
Home Safety
Firework Safety
Electrical Fires
Fire Prevention

MUSIC: Electrical Fires
Fire Prevention

ART & DESIGN: Emergency
Home Safety
Firework Safety
Electrical Fires
Fire Prevention

ICT: Emergency
Firework Safety

FIRE SAFETY

PERSONAL AND COMMUNITY SAFETY

PURPOSE:
- **To provide children with a better understanding of community issues and how they can be involved.**
- **To build up a wider knowledge of personal and community safety within their own experience and beyond.**
- **To encourage individual thinking and decision making.**

FACT: Never talk to strangers. If approached by one say no, run and shout at the top of your voice.

FACT: 36,000 children undergo treatment from poisoning by household items such as bleach, white spirit and paint stripper.

FACT: 59% of all UK accidental deaths by drowning were in open areas of water.

Page 27	**STRANGERS**
Page 28	**ACCIDENTS AT HOME**
Page 29	**RAIL SAFETY**
Page 30	**COUNTRYSIDE AND FARM SAFETY**
Page 31	**WATER SAFETY**
Page 32	**SAFETY ON THE STREETS**
Page 33	**KEY LINKS CHART**

TEACHER'S NOTE:
RESOURCES FOR PERSONAL & COMMUNITY SAFETY INCLUDE:
- Play Safe, Stay Safe, Keep Safe (7-11 years)
- Junior Citizen Handbook (7-11 years)
- Respect Your Life Your Choice (11-14 years)
- The Young Person's Guide To Bullying (7-11 years)
- Out and About (7-11 years)

STRANGERS

PURPOSE: To make children aware of the dangers of talking to and going with strangers.

TEACHER INFORMATION:

Over the past few years there has been an increase in the number of child abductions and attacks. It is very important, therefore, that children know and understand what to do if approached by a stranger.

They should let an adult who is at home know where they are going and what time they will be back. Also they should tell the adult who they are with.

It is dangerous to play near car parks, ponds, in empty buildings, on rubbish dumps and scrap yards.

Remember, a stranger is someone you don't know well. Many strangers are completely innocent but there are some who are very bad. It is therefore a good idea not to talk to any strangers.

Always tell children to stay in a group and not to go off on their own.

They should not use dark alleyways or unlit routes. They must always choose a safe route.

Get them to learn their own phone number off by heart and if they are being picked up from school to have a family password.

STRANGER DANGERS
- Never take sweets from a stranger.
- Always keep a distance between them and their car.
- If children feel in danger then go to someone you know or a police officer.
- Strangers will sometimes tell lies. If someone suspicious starts to come towards a child, tell them to make for a large group of people making sure that they tell someone what has happened.

KEY ACTIVITY (E)
YOU WILL NEED: crayons, card, group of friends.

Make up a short story about being approached by a stranger. What should you do? Hold up a poster at the end of the play saying **'If in doubt shout.'**

FURTHER IDEAS:
- Work out some short 'stranger' plays with a variety of different endings. (E)
- Create your own personal list of emergency phone numbers in case you need to get help. (M)
- Find out what you can about Banardos and what happened to children in Victorian times. (H)
- Make a set of 'Stranger Danger' signs. (A)
- Draw a plan of your area and mark in any areas that are dangerous. (M)
- Investigate what happens to us when we get frightened. Find out about adrenaline and also why we sometimes perspire if we become very anxious. (S)
- Find out what you can about organisations that help children in distress. e.g. Kidscape, Childline. (ICT)

PERSONAL & COMMUNITY SAFETY

ACCIDENTS AT HOME

PURPOSE: To get the children to recognise a variety of different potential dangers in the home.

TEACHER INFORMATION:
Accidents tend to happen at home. Some of the most common causes are:

- **ELECTROCUTION:** Never use electrical equipment in the bathroom. Never mess about with plugs and sockets. Never overload sockets.
- **DROWNING:** Never leave young children near water. It takes just 3 centimetres of water for a baby to drown.
- **BURNS:** Children should never play with matches. Adults should never leave lit cigarettes or pipes unattended. Pans of hot water or fat are extremely dangerous.
- **CHOKING:** Young children like to put things in their mouths and can choke on very small items such as a peanut or a bead. Plastic bags can also be very dangerous and cause suffocation.
- **POISONING:** Kitchen cupboards can contain a host of chemicals and medicines which have brightly coloured labels. Many of these are harmful such as:

Ammonia	Aftershave
Bleach	Caustic soda
Firelighters	Insecticide
Window cleaner	Oven cleaner
Paint	Petrol
Shampoo	Slug pellets
Toilet cleaner	Washing powder
Weed killer	

Some of the most common causes of child deaths by poisoning are white spirit, paintstripper, and lavatory cleaner. Around 36,000 children undergo treatment for poisoning every year. Most of these are under three and most accidents happen in the home.

- **FALLS:** These often happen when you climb onto something or trip. The bathroom is a very common place for this to happen.

KEY ACTIVITY (E)
YOU WILL NEED: pencil, paper.

Write a story based on a toddler left at home for the day. Look at the things that might happen to them and the dangers they might face.

FURTHER IDEAS:
- Design some safety labels for a range of household products. (DT,A)
- Work out a dance/drama piece which uses your own music to tell the story of a near death by poisoning. (E, Ms)
- Design your own safe house, then make a model of it. (DT,A)
- Investigate what kind of home accidents happen in your area. Produce a graph to show your results. (M)
- Design some home safety posters. (A)
- Find out what some household products are made of. (S)

RAIL SAFETY

PURPOSE: To recognise some of the major dangers on the rail network.

TEACHER INFORMATION:

Railways can be extremely dangerous places and children need to be warned not to play on them or near them. Every year a number of children get killed or injured on them. Accidents also occur at railway stations. These can be caused by people being knocked onto the track and people falling from platforms. Standing near the edge of the platform when high speed trains come through is also very dangerous.

It can take a high speed train around a mile and a half to stop. The warning lights at level crossings should always be obeyed and if the gates close it means that a train will be coming through very soon. It is against the law to play near railway lines. Some lines carry very fast trains whilst others are electrified and carry around 25,000 volts. It is not necessary to touch a rail to be killed as electricity can jump. This electricity is never switched off.

This is a set of guidelines from the British Transport Police:

- Never go onto a railway line.
- Never damage any of the fences and report any damage that you see.
- Do not use a skateboard, roller blades or a bike on a station platform.
- Never open a train door until it has completely stopped.
- Stand well back from the edge of platforms.
- Do not put your hand or arm out of a train window.
- Never throw anything at a train, put things on the line or hang things from bridges.
- Always obey all the signs.
- Do not go over a level crossing when the barriers are down.

Throwing things onto the tracks and damaging the rails is one of the most serious problems on the railways and underground systems.

KEY ACTIVITY (M)

YOU WILL NEED: Rail timetables, pencil, paper, calculator.
Plan a journey from your nearest station to a big city such as London, Manchester or Glasgow. Work out the times you will need to leave and any connections you will need to make. Draw a map showing your route. See if you can find out the return fare. What is the cheapest fare you can get? (G)

FURTHER IDEAS:

- Find out how a modern train works. Draw some pictures and diagrams to explain the different parts. (S)
- Make a visit to a local railway museum. (H,S)
- Write to the local railway company or the British Transport Police and ask if they will come in and talk about safety on the railways. (E)
- Surf the Internet for information on other railway networks around the world. (ICT)
- Write a story based on a railway journey. (E)
- See what you can find out about Eurostar. Where does it go and what kind of train is it? (G,S)

PERSONAL & COMMUNITY SAFETY

COUNTRYSIDE AND FARM SAFETY

PURPOSE: To understand some of the dangers that can be found in rural areas and on farms as well as learning to respect the countryside.

TEACHER INFORMATION:

Children should learn to respect the countryside and understand that it should be left undamaged. There is a countryside code which should be followed:

1. Respect and enjoy the countryside.
2. Guard against fires.
3. Shut and fasten all gates.
4. Use gates and stiles for crossing walls, hedges and fences.
5. Protect wildlife, trees and plants.
6. Take care on country roads.
7. Take your litter home.
8. Keep your dog under close control.
9. Keep to public footpaths across farmland.
10. Do not make a lot of noise.
11. Do not touch livestock, machinery and crops.

It is vital that in rural areas children are aware of water. Rivers, ponds and lakes can be very deep and the water cold. If they do fall in they should be calm and try to float on their backs. If they can they should attract attention by waving an arm. If someone they are with falls in the water they should not attempt to go into the water but reach out with something such as a stick or piece of rope.
They should call the emergency services as soon as possible.

Dangers to watch for in and around farms include:

- Areas where animals are kept.
- Farm machinery. Tractors and also machines that plough and sow.
- Chemicals and fuels. These are often kept in farmyards.
- Barns. These can contain large amounts of hay which can be dangerous.
- Silos used for grain.
- Areas storing animal waste and manure and also slurry pits.

KEY ACTIVITY (E)

YOU WILL NEED: paper, pencil, crayons.
Make up your own Farm Code based on the kind of dangers you think you might come across in and around farms. Produce a farm safety poster.

FURTHER IDEAS:

- Make up a play about the dangers of going near farm machinery. (E)
- See if you can find out the longest river in Britain and then the world. How long are they? Make up a table of the worlds 5 longest rivers. (G,M)
- Arrange a class visit to a local farm and/or to the countryside for the day. Remember to use the country code. (G)
- Create some watery pictures. (A)
- Why are rules necessary in the countryside? Discuss. (E)
- Write a story or report about a trip with the family to a lake or farm. (E)
- Draw a picture of a piece of farm machinery and write down why it could be dangerous. (A,E)

PERSONAL & COMMUNITY SAFETY

WATER SAFETY

PURPOSE: To respect the water and areas such as the seaside, rivers and ponds.

TEACHER INFORMATION:
There are a large number of accidents every year in ponds, lakes, and at the seaside. If you see an emergency at the seaside then you should dial 999 and ask for the coastguard. They work alongside the police and the other emergency services.

Many children visit the seaside every year and so it is important for them to understand that although it can be fun, there are also a number of dangers.

Flags are often flown to indicate the state of the water;

RED   You must not go in the water.
YELLOW   Dangerous for the young and the old.
GREEN   Safe to swim, but take care.
RED AND YELLOW STRIPED
Safe to swim in this area, lifeguard on patrol.

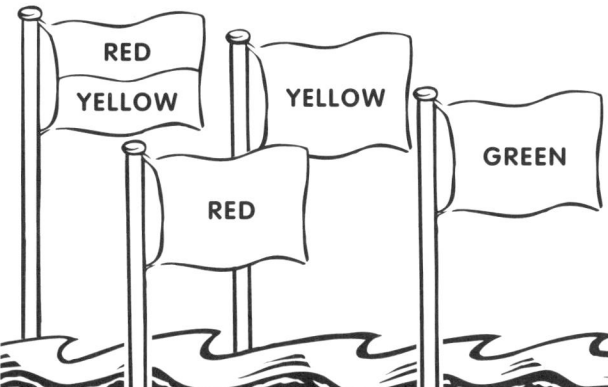

SEASIDE CODE:
- Make sure that you know what the weather is going to be like. It can change very quickly at the seaside.
- Don't attempt to climb up cliffs or slippery rocks.
- Be very careful when in small boats, rubber dingys and on airbeds.
- Be careful of the tide.
- If anyone is in trouble dial 999 for assistance.

Ponds, rivers and canals can be dangerous with strong undercurrents and dirty water. If you are going near water it is a good idea to go with an adult.

Garden ponds can also be a hazard to very young children. Fencing off a pond is often the only way of making sure young children are safe. Any fencing should be properly fixed as very young children can easily crawl underneath it.

59% of all UK accidental deaths by drowning (1999) were in open areas of water whilst only 125 were in swimming pools and usually associated with a medical condition.

KEY ACTIVITY (H, DT)
YOU WILL NEED: paper, pencil, colours.

Make up a booklet about the history of the coastguard service or the RNLI (Royal National Lifeboat Institution) who provide voluntary lifeboats around our coastline. If you have an RNLI station in your area then find out more about the people that run it.

FURTHER IDEAS:
- Invite a coastguard or person who works on a lifeboat to come in and talk about their jobs. (E)
- Find out the kind of creatures that might live along the seashore. (G)
- Who is your local water company? Write to them and see if they have any material on water safety. (E)
- Make up a song about the dangers of playing near water. (Ms)
- Produce a safety poster based on the kind of dangers you might find around a canal. (A)

SAFETY ON THE STREETS

PURPOSE: To investigate how to remain safe on the streets.

TEACHER INFORMATION:

In olden days the streets of our cities could be dangerous places. In medieval times rubbish would have been thrown out of windows directly onto the paths. There were no sewers and so waste just piled up on the footpaths and roads. Pickpockets would have been around and also muggers waiting in dark corners to attack people. The streets would have been filled with animals and vehicles. Wooden houses would have posed a fire risk and stray animals would have been seen around the streets.

Today the dangers include unknown strangers, muggers and pickpockets and extremely busy roads. Litter can still be a problem with overflowing waste bins. Vandalism and graffiti can be seen on bus shelters and the sides of buildings. Cars are constantly being stolen by joyriders and people wanting to use them for robberies and acts of violence.

- When children go out to play they need to tell an adult where they are going and the time they will be back.
- They should go out in groups rather than on their own.
- They should never play in dangerous areas.
- They should be careful of the traffic.
- They need to be able to make their own decisions and report any bad behaviour by others.
- They should cross the road if they see people they don't feel comfortable with.
- They should go out at different times during the day so that people cannot predict their movements.
- If they see a crime being committed they need to note down as many details as possible. Not to get involved but remember what they see. If the information they give to the police is accurate then it will useful.

Some things to remember:

PEOPLE:	**VEHICLES:**
Male or female?	What was it?
Age?	Make/Model?
Colour of skin?	Colour?
Hair?	Registration Number?
Clothing?	Which way did it go?
Anything unusual about them?	Who was driving it?

If they are out on the streets they need to be alert. They may see someone interfering with a car or passing small packages to someone else. They need to remember to be alert at all times.

KEY ACTIVITY (E, M)

YOU WILL NEED: a tray, ten items, cloth, pencil, paper.

Put ten items on a tray and cover it with a cloth. Put the tray in front of a friend and uncover it for one minute. Cover it again. Now get them to write down as many items as they can remember. If they manage to remember all ten, ask them to tell you the colour and size etc. of each thing. See how many things they can remember. Try this with five people and then record your results.

FURTHER IDEAS:

- Have a discussion on whether or not the class thinks that there are more dangers on your streets today than say 200 years ago. (E)
- Who were the Bow Street Runners and the Peelers? Make some investigation on how crime used to be dealt with 150 years ago? (H)
- Devise some methods of protecting cars from thieves and joyriders. (E,DT)
- Draw some people acting suspiciously. (A)
- Produce your own 'Street Awareness Code'. (E)
- Invite a local police officer to come in and talk about being 'Street Aware'. (E)

KEY LINKS

MATHEMATICS:
Strangers
Accidents In The Home
Rail Safety
Countryside And Farm Safety
Safety On The Streets

ENGLISH:
Strangers
Accidents In The Home
Rail Safety
Countryside And Farm Safety
Water Safety
Safety On The Streets

SCIENCE:
Strangers
Accidents In The Home
Rail Safety

HISTORY:
Strangers
Rail Safety
Water Safety
Safety On The Streets

GEOGRAPHY:
Rail Safety
Fire Safety
Water Safety

DESIGN AND TECHNOLOGY:
Accidents In The Home
Water Safety
Safety On The Streets

MUSIC:
Accidents In The Home
Water Safety

ART & DESIGN:
Strangers
Accidents In The Home
Countryside And Farm Safety
Safety On The Streets

ICT:
Strangers
Rail Safety

PERSONAL & COMMUNITY SAFETY

BULLYING

PURPOSE:
- To provide background information and look at a variety of issues surrounding bullying.
- To build up a wider knowledge of bullying within their own experience and beyond.
- To encourage individual thinking and decision making.

FACT: Bullying can be carried out by verbal, physical abuse and silent bullying.

FACT: Adults can be bullied at work.

Page 35	**HOW DOES IT WORK?**
Page 36	**CAUSES OF BULLYING**
Page 37	**BEING ASSERTIVE**
Page 38	**CONFRONTING BULLYING**
Page 39	**BEATING THE BULLIES**
Page 40	**A SURVEY ON BULLYING**
Page 41	**KEY LINKS CHART**

TEACHER'S NOTE:
RESOURCES FOR BULLYING INCLUDE:
- Junior Citizen Handbook (7-11 years)
- Play Safe, Stay Safe, Keep Safe (7-11 years)
- The Young Person's Guide To Bullying (7-11 years)

HOW DOES IT WORK?

PURPOSE: To investigate how bullying occurs.

TEACHER INFORMATION:
Bullying occurs when someone sets out to hurt another individual. This can be a child or an adult. The idea is to make them feel unhappy and even scared. This is often done physically and also mentally.

PHYSICAL BULLYING:
This is when someone is punched, hit, kicked or attacked. Bullies operate in clever ways and will accidentally bang into someone or trip them over. They can operate on their own or in groups.

VERBAL BULLYING:
Bullies can threaten people or call them names. They may taunt the victim or repeat what they say in a silly voice. They will sometimes humiliate them by making them look stupid.

SILENT BULLYING:
This is when they ignore you or try and stop you from joining in. They may send an individual to 'Coventry'. Rumours can be spread and if you have a mobile phone they may send you 'hate' text messages. Sometimes they will continually follow you around.

Bullying often happens between people who are not friends (however this is not always the case) the victim has no choice. Bullies tend to like repeating things and going on about their achievements.

A bully is someone who likes to feel powerful. Their victim may be someone who is different or lacks confidence.

Bullying can happen in or out of school, when someone is in the playground or on their way home.

Bullies need people to keep quiet. They cannot afford to let their victims tell others who can help what is wrong.

KEY ACTIVITY (E)
YOU WILL NEED: pencil, paper.

Get a group of friends to each make their own list of things that bullies do to frighten their victims. Once the lists are completed compare them. After a discussion make a final list of ten things that bullies do based upon the results of the group.

FURTHER IDEAS:
- What is the difference between teasing, mucking about and real bullying? Discuss. (E)
- See if you can find any stories or tales about people who are bullied. (E)
- Write a day in the life of someone who is being bullied. (E)
- Which of these phrases are true?
  - Bullies come in all shapes and sizes.
  - Bullies get their own way by making someone feel bad.
  - Bullies need their victims to be afraid of them.
  - Bullies are popular in class.
  - Bullies like to prove how strong they are.
  - Bullies sometimes go around in gangs.
  - Bullies are usually quiet people.
  - You can always tell who is a bully just by looking at them. (E)

BULLYING

CAUSES OF BULLYING

PURPOSE: To discuss the root causes of bullying and look at who gets bullied.

TEACHER INFORMATION:
Bullies like to pick on certain types of individuals. These may include children who are:

VULNERABLE
New to the school: They won't have made new friends, may not know who to go to for help and may feel uncertain because things are new.

Younger or smaller: Bullies usually pick on children who are smaller or weaker than themselves.

Lonely: These may be children who find it difficult to make friends for a variety of reasons. They are a good target for a bully as they won't have very many friends to turn to for help.

Having problems: Children who might feel let down for some reason or are having difficulties at home are an easy target as they may be feeling low and find it difficult to stand up for themselves.

PASSIVE
The victims of bullying are often passive and find it difficult to defend themselves in an argument. Passive children may come from homes where there is very little shouting and they don't know what to do. They may come from a family where they are bossed about and haven't yet learnt how to stick up for themselves. Passive individuals tend not to stand up to bullies and so get picked on over and over again.

Some children are picked on just because they are different. It may be their looks, their personality or their interests. It is important that children learn that each person is an individual and unique. The world would be a very boring place if we were all the same. It is the diversity of cultures, personalities and interests that makes the world such an interesting and exciting place. Sometimes a bully will pick on people like this because they are jealous of them.

There are a number of reasons why a person may become a bully.
- They may always get their own way.
- They come from a home where they argue and fight a lot.
- They get bullied themselves.
- Something nasty has happened to them and they need to take their anger out on someone.
- They haven't any friends and don't know any other way to communicate with people.
- They are frightened of life and have to act tough.
- They are always being told that they have to be the best at everything.
- Although they may be unhappy themselves it is wrong that they should try and take it out on someone else.

KEY ACTIVITY (E)
YOU WILL NEED: pencil, paper.

Think about your best friend. Write down all the things that you like about them. How are they different to you. Why do you like them/what have you learnt from them?

FURTHER IDEAS:
- Make a large collage of faces. Get each person to draw the face of someone else in the class. When they are finished stick them onto a large piece of paper and mount it on the wall. How are the children in the class similar to each other? (A.E)
- Which of these words may describe: **1.** A bully, **2.** A victim :-
  sad, angry, passive, nervous, jealous, timid, afraid, frightened, thoughtless. (E)
- Design and paint a poster on the topic of stopping bullies. (A)
- Make up a play about a child who is bullied, stops the person bullying them and then, in the end, becomes their friend. (E)
- Write a poem on bullying or a news report on a bully who eventually ends up at the police station because of their actions. (E)

BEING ASSERTIVE

PURPOSE: To look at ways in which you can be more assertive and stand up to bullies.

TEACHER INFORMATION:

Assertive people usually stick up for themselves and feel confident. They tend to like themselves and understand their own feelings. It is sometimes difficult to be assertive if someone is being horrible to you as you may be feeling sad or angry.

Assertive people know:
- What is important to them.
- What it is to like themselves.
- When to say no.
- How to ask for things they want.
- How to deal with anger.

Get the children to think about their good points. It is important to remember that we cannot all be good at everything. Get them to think about their favourite pastimes, why people like them and the things that they are doing. What has been the most important event in their lives?

When faced with a bully you need to assert yourself. You should make eye contact with the person, not smile and just say no. Stay with a group rather than be on your own. If possible walk away from the situation. Think positively, and tell an adult what has happened. However make sure that it is someone you can trust.

Assertiveness comes from being able to :
- Ask for what you want.
- Know how to say no.
- Understand anger.

KEY ACTIVITY (E)
YOU WILL NEED: pencil, paper.

Write down an incident in your life when you got angry because you were treated really badly. Looking back on this event was there any other way you could have handled it? Draw a series of cartoon pictures to illustrate what happened and write down a brief description of what is happening in each picture.

FURTHER IDEAS:
- Discuss what makes people angry? Is there anything they can do to calm themselves? Is it possible to be angry and yet in control? (E)
- Get the children to draw a picture of something that makes them angry yet still in control. (A)
- Are there any environmental issues in the local area that are causing problems and making people upset? How might bullies operate in situations like this? (G)
- Draw a picture of yourself and write down by the side, ways in which you can be assertive. (A)
- Think up ways someone might be able to ask for the following.

    a. To change the channel on the television set.
    b. To borrow your brother's football boots or your sister's top.
    c. For your pen back from someone who has borrowed it for a long time.
    d. Your bag back if it has been taken by someone who is acting like a bully. (E)

CONFRONTING BULLYING

PURPOSE: To examine further ways in which children may be able to confront bullies.

TEACHER INFORMATION:
There are number of ways children can deal with bullying:
- Always stay with a crowd as they will be less likely to be approached.
- Keep in sight of an adult particularly at playtimes.
- Look confident.
- Always ask for help. Talk to parents, carers or the teacher.
- Keep a diary of events. Write down what happens, where and when.
- See if there are any witnesses who would be able to tell an adult what happened.
- Practice their replies and comments.
- Learn some self defence moves. These will make them feel more confident and may help them out of a difficult situation.

If they get into a situation where they are being bullied they should try some of these ideas:
- Walk away if they can.
- Try to talk their way out of it. Only do this if they are good with words or can make people laugh easily.
- Keep cool. Don't argue. Bullies really like arguments.
- Stand tall. Look as though they are not scared.
- If they are harassed by a gang look for the weakest person and tell them they are not going to be bullied anymore.
- Say no to them and walk away at once.
- If they are in a gang where there is bullying going on they should try and stop it. Remember as part of a gang everyone is responsible. If bullying continues they should leave the gang at once and go and get help.

They may think that their sister or brother is being bullied. The signs are that they:
- Hate to go to certain places.
- Cry at night or in private.
- Feel sick and unhappy at the same time every week.
- They are losing things.
- They have bruises and cuts they can't explain.
- They have suddenly become quiet or had a personality change.

In cases such as this they should be a good listener. Remember as an individual they must not give in to bullying.

KEY ACTIVITY (E)
YOU WILL NEED: pencil, paper.
How would you help someone out who is being bullied? Write down some of your suggestions.

FURTHER IDEAS:
- What could you say to a bully? (E)
- Make a list of people you could talk to about someone you know who is being bullied. (E)
- Write a song or rap about how to combat bullying and add some instrumental music to your piece. (Ms)
- Invite someone in from a local organisation that deals with bullying and get them to talk to the class about ways in which you can fight against it. (E)
- Write a letter to an aunt or uncle telling them how you were able to fight against a local bully and win. (E)

BEATING THE BULLIES

PURPOSE: To discuss ways in which children can work together to stop people bullying them.

TEACHER INFORMATION:

Discuss with the children the various ways in which the school could work together to stamp out bullying.

Talk about where bullying might take place e.g. in quiet places or dark corners away from staff, on the way home from school.

It may be possible to launch an anti-bullying campaign in the school with an assembly or poster campaign.

The children might like to create a bully buster organisation to try and stop bullies from operating.

Discuss some of the following situations with them:

- Someone accidentally trips you over on the way home. What do you do?

- You are in a quiet corner of the playground, a gang comes up and one of them punches you really hard and then tells you not to say anything 'or else'. What do you do?

- A new child joins the class. Some people make fun of them because they have a different accent to the rest of the class. What do you do?

KEY ACTIVITY (M)
YOU WILL NEED: paper, pencil.

Carry out a survey about bullying and how often it happens. All the information you receive should be anonymous. Present your results as a graph or chart. You could then make suggestions on ways to stop it such as checking quiet areas, opening up and lighting quiet and dark corners.

FURTHER IDEAS:

- Make up some playground games that are fun, get everyone to join in. (PE)

- Carry out a survey on what people do at playtimes. What games do they play, who do they talk to? What kind of improvements can be made? (E)

- Introduce a selection of co-operative games where lots of people take part. (PE)

- Decide to make something as a group of five or as an individual e.g. a simple puppet. If you are working as a group give each person a different task. See how many puppets a group of five can make in one hour and how many five individuals can make. Discuss the problems and advantages of working in a group or as individuals. (E)

BULLYING

A SURVEY ON BULLYING

If you have ever been bullied, fill in the page. What did the bully do?

Photocopy the survey and quietly answer the questions but do not put your name on it. Your teacher may read some of them out.

SOMEBODY...	NOT AT ALL	ONCE	MORE THAN ONCE
Called me names			
Said something nice to me			
Was nasty about my family			
Tried to kick me			
Was unkind because I am different			
Was rude about the colour of my skin			
Said they'd beat me up			
Tried to make me hurt other people			
Tried to hurt me			
Made me do something I didn't want to			
Smiled at me			
Tried to get me into trouble			
Laughed at me horribly			
Shouted at me			
Sent me a nasty text message			

BULLYING

KEY LINKS

MATHEMATICS: Beating the Bullies

ENGLISH: How Does It Work?
What Causes Bullying?
Beating the Bullies
Being Assertive
Confronting Bullying

SCIENCE:

HISTORY:

GEOGRAPHY: Being Assertive

DESIGN AND TECHNOLOGY:

MUSIC: Confronting Bullying

ART & DESIGN: What Causes Bullying?
Being Assertive

ICT:

BULLYING

HATE CRIME

PURPOSE:
- **To understand the meaning of the term and to look at ways of combating it.**
- **To encourage individual thinking and decision making.**

FACT: It is illegal to use racist abuse. The Race Relations Act was passed in 1976 and then had its powers strengthened in 2001.

FACT: The police take all types of hate crime very seriously.

Page 43	**LEGAL RIGHTS**
Page 44	**MY RIGHTS**
Page 45	**RACISM AND SEXISM**
Page 46	**P.L.A.N.**
Page 47	**HATE CRIME**
Page 48	**WHAT ARE WE GOING TO DO?**
Page 49	**KEY LINKS CHART**

TEACHER'S NOTE:
RESOURCES FOR HATE CRIME INCLUDE:
- Junior Citizen Handbook (7-11 years)
- Play Safe, Stay Safe, Keep Safe (7-11 years)
- The Young Person's Guide To Bullying (7-11 years)

LEGAL RIGHTS

PURPOSE: To consider children's legal rights.

TEACHER INFORMATION:

Talk to the children about what they think their rights are. Explain that some of our rights are laws. Discuss with them some of the rights that they consider they might have.

Here are a few that you might like to consider:

- Can they have a building society or bank account.
- Can they get married?
- Can they buy cigarettes?
- Do they have to go to school?
- Can they drive a car or a motorcycle?
- Can they have their own passport?
- Can they drink in a pub?
- Can they buy a pet?

Talk about the legal rights of adults as well as children.

Discuss human rights with them. Rights are things that everyone should have. The right to shelter, food and water. Because we live in a country where we have rights we must remember that we also have responsibilities.

Think about the different rights that you might have.

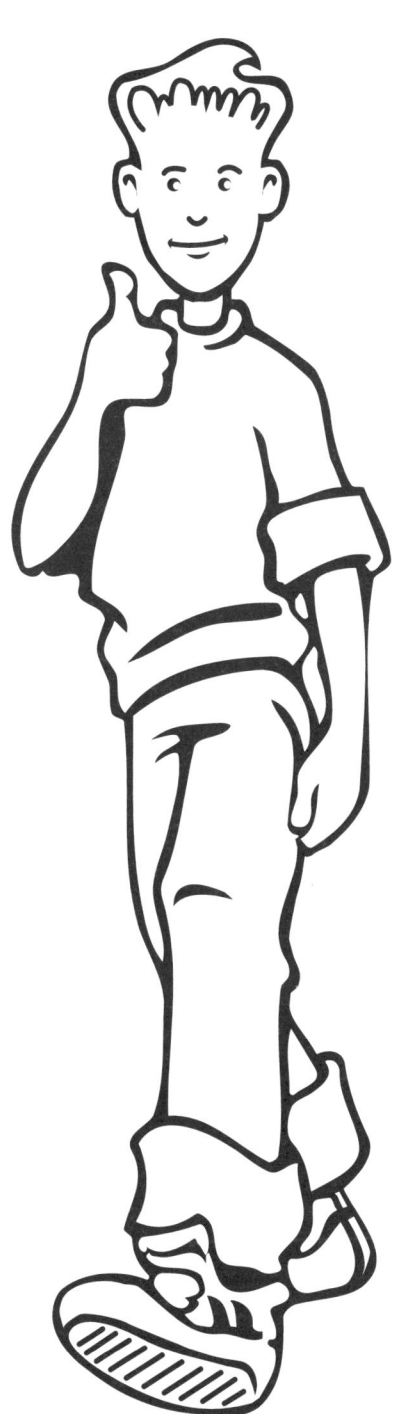

KEY ACTIVITY (E)
YOU WILL NEED: pencil, paper.

If you were going to produce your own Bill of Rights what would be included in it?

FURTHER IDEAS:

- What happens if people's legal rights are taken away from them? (E)
- What kind of services do we get in this country which are provided by the Government? (E)

HATE CRIME

MY RIGHTS

PURPOSE: To consider children's rights at school and home.

TEACHER INFORMATION:

Talk about what kind of rights children might have at school and what rights they would like. What rights have we got as individuals?

Discuss with them the feasibility of some of their ideas e.g. would it be a good idea if they could just walk in and out of the classroom when they wanted to, bring their bicycles into the classroom, or cook their own meals at school?

Talk about the possibility of a school council. What purpose would it serve? How would it work? What kind of decisions could or should be made by class representatives that were members?

What kind of rights should they have at home? e.g. switch channels on the television whenever they felt like it? Eat what they like when they like? Why are some of these rights not practical?

KEY ACTIVITY (E)

YOU WILL NEED: pencil, paper.

Put these rights in order with the most important one first. Are any of them not workable?

The right to:

- Sit anywhere in the classroom.
- Bring your own chair to school.
- Go to lunch at any time.
- Wear what you like for school.
- Make as much noise as you like in class.
- Eat and drink in class.
- Stay in at playtime.
- Go out to play when you feel like it.
- Have somewhere in the class to put your things.
- Have a kind and considerate teacher.
- Discuss each right as you go along.

FURTHER IDEAS:

- Make a large poster with ten class rules on it. What happens if people break the rules? (A,E)
- Make up a list of ten rights you think all children should have when at home. (E)
- Investigate rights issues and look at some people who stood up for what they believed in e.g. Martin Luther King, Emily Pankhurst, Nelson Mandella. (H)

HATE CRIME

RACISM AND SEXISM

PURPOSE: To extend the children's knowledge of racism and sexism and discuss the possible consequences.

TEACHER INFORMATION:

Racism and sexism are two problems which may come up at school or be brought into school from outside.

Racism is often caused by people who believe that the colour of your skin makes you better than someone else. This can cause a great deal of trouble and upset. It is important to remember that we are all individuals from different backgrounds and cultures. No race is any better than any other.

At school racism can be caused by bullying, teasing people about the way they dress and the way they talk. It can be teasing about the way they look or the way they move.

Outside school racial abuse can include attacks at football matches, on people's homes, on individuals in the street or in their homes. It is also caused by ignorance.

Children and adults have the right to live in a world free from racial abuse, harassment and discrimination.

Threatening or insulting behaviour is against the law and taken very seriously by the police.

It is important that we do not judge people just on their appearance or colour of their skin. People have personalities and characters and these matter a great deal.

Some people also discriminate against others because of their sex. Girls or boys are often considered not good enough to do certain things. This is also wrong. Everyone should be treated as equals and given the same opportunities as others.

What would someone feel like if they had been racially abused?
Maybe hated and despised, maybe even hating their own culture.

What is racism doing to all of us? Spreading hate and violence, causing people and races to argue and fight against each other and even with each other. Stopping us living peacefully together, stopping us achieving what we are capable of at school and outside, frightening us?

KEY ACTIVITY (E)

YOU WILL NEED: pencil, paper.

Make a list of things that you could do to stamp out racism or sexism in your school or local area.

FURTHER IDEAS:

- Discuss why you need to be a good listener. (E)
- What kind of words do you like to be used when someone is talking to you? Are any of them special words? (E)
- Invite in a parent with an Asian, African or Far Eastern background to talk about some of the festivals they celebrate during the year. (G)
- Organise some multicultral cooking sessions. Investigate a range of simple hot and cold dishes. These could be themed e.g. Indian, Mediterranean, South American, African. (M)
- Develop an anti-racism or anti-sexist campaign in the school. (E)
- What kind of things could be done to make life more equal for boys and girls in school? (E)

HATE CRIME

P.L.A.N.

PURPOSE: To inform children of P.L.A.N. and to teach how it works.

TEACHER INFORMATION:
Children will feel safer if they teach themselves to **P.L.A.N.** before they go anywhere.

PREPARE. They should think how to get somewhere and how to get back. They should tell someone before they go, who they are going with and when they are back, thinking about the dangers when they are out.

LOOK confident and let someone know where you are going. Wear comfortable clothes and shoes so you can move easily. Remember your body language and to look tall and look like you know where you are going and why. Carry a shriek alarm and know how to use it. Have a list of emergency numbers with you and some change in your pocket if you do not have a mobile phone. Remember to put keys somewhere safe.

AVOID risks and be aware of what is happening/keep looking and listening to what is going on around you. Keep away from unknown places. Try not to change your plans at the last minute. If you do, tell someone. Always keep one hand free.

NEVER take safety for granted. Never say to yourself it only happens to other people or it's only a short journey or they look honest.

Whatever you are going to do you will be safer and more confident if you remember to **P.L.A.N.** first.

Children should remember to trust their instincts and if they feel something is wrong, take action to avoid the danger.

KEY ACTIVITY (M, E)
YOU WILL NEED: pencil, large piece of paper, ruler.

Draw out your route from home to school. Mark any danger spots in red and colour the safest part of your route in green.

FURTHER IDEAS:

- What kind of things can you do to protect yourself when you're out in the dark at night? (E)
- What would you do if you were spoken to by a stranger in a car with its engine running? (E)
- Design some clothing that would be useful in the dark. (DT)
- Carry out some tests using a variety of different torches. Which were the best in the dark? Why? (S)
- Make a list of people who you could contact in an emergency. (E)
- Which of these places do you think would be safest to go to if you were at risk at night and why?... public house, empty bus shelter, park, derelict house, police station, garage, public toilet. (E)
- Make up a short play about being scared and going for help. (E)

HATE CRIME

HATE CRIME

PURPOSE: To explain hate crime and ways of stamping it out.

TEACHER INFORMATION:

Hate Crime is often a result of ignorance or insensitivity. It can be very harmful and is very wrong. It is important that we do not treat someone who is different from us in a totally negative way, in a way that we would not want to be treated.

Hate Crime can have a terrible effect on the victim who can feel hated and despised and even end up hating their own people.

It spreads hate and violence throughout the community and often divides people and those living peacefully. It also stops people from doing their best either at school or at work.

Everyone has the right to live without discrimination. Remember if you are discriminated against it is not your fault, you are not to blame.

If you know someone who is suffering from hate crime then listen to them. Take the matter seriously and be prepared to tell someone such as a teacher or the police. Your friend may be too scared or upset. You can report hate crimes to the police without giving your name. Never join in with bullies.

Make sure the school has a list of helplines to be used in cases of hate crime.

Find out how your friends like to be known and what words they use. Teach these to parents, carers, and grandparents.

KEY ACTIVITY (DT, E)

YOU WILL NEED: pencil, large piece of paper, ruler.

Make a large anti-hate crime poster for display in the school, use bright colours, make the message short and to the point. Get your message across.

FURTHER IDEAS:

- Write out the main points of P.L.A.N. then make some P.L.A.N. leaflets. (DT,A,E)
- Make up a cartoon type strip telling the story of someone who is subject to hate crime and how you and a group of friends solve the problem. (E,A)
- Produce a list of adults who you could go to if you thought that hate crime was taking place in or around your school. (E)
- Make up a song, poem or rap about how to fight hate crime. (Ms,E)
- Link up with a school in Asia, Africa or the Far East via the Internet. Find out about each other's schools. (ICT)
- Search for 'Charter of Human Rights' on the Internet. (ICT)

WHAT ARE WE GOING TO DO?

Tim has a problem. He is being bullied. Can you finish off this cartoon strip and find ways to stop the bullies?

HATE CRIME

KEY LINKS

MATHEMATICS: Racism And Sexism
P.L.A.N.

ENGLISH: Legal Rights
My Rights
Racism And Sexism
P.L.A.N.
Hate Crime

SCIENCE: P.L.A.N.

HISTORY: My Rights

GEOGRAPHY: Racism And Sexism

DESIGN AND TECHNOLOGY: P.L.A.N.
Hate Crime

MUSIC: Hate Crime

ART & DESIGN: My Rights
Hate Crime

PE:

ICT: Hate Crime

HEALTH EDUCATION

PURPOSE:
- **To make children aware of a range of facts on smoking, alcohol and drugs and to discuss a range of issues.**
- **To help build up a wider knowledge of these issues in the immediate area and further afield.**
- **To encourage individual thinking and decision making.**

FACT: The Health Service spends in the region of £500 million each year on smoking related illnesses.

FACT: Adults are legally allowed to smoke and drink.

Page 51	**SMOKING - THE FACTS**
Page 52	**SAYING NO TO SMOKING**
Page 53	**ALCOHOL - THE FACTS**
Page 54	**THE DANGERS OF ALCOHOL**
Page 55	**DRUGS THAT HELP**
Page 56	**DRUG ABUSE**
Page 57	**KEY LINKS CHART**

TEACHER'S NOTE:
RESOURCES FOR HEALTH EDUCATION INCLUDE:
- Will Power's Beware (7-11 years)
- Play Safe, Stay Safe, Keep Safe (7-11 years)
- Junior Citizen Handbook (7-11 years)
- Respect Your Life, Your Choice (11-14 years)

SMOKING - THE FACTS

PURPOSE: To explain the facts about smoking.

TEACHER INFORMATION:

In Great Britain around 450 children start smoking every day. It is illegal to sell any tobacco product to anyone under the age of 16. Tobacco contains over 4,000 chemicals in the form of particles and gases.

More than 17,000 children under the age of five are admitted to hospital every year because of passive smoking. Passive smoking can cause dizziness, headache, cough, sore throat or nausea.

Around 600 people die of lung cancer every year due to passive smoking. One fifth of all deaths in the UK every year are linked in some way to smoking.

Smoking makes rooms and clothing smell. It pollutes the atmosphere and it also may cause fires.

In the UK every packet of cigarettes has a health warning on it. Tobacco companies are also not allowed to advertise on television.

It has been found that some children as young as five smoke!

Unborn babies are put at great risk if their mothers smoke.

KEY ACTIVITY (H, ICT)

YOU WILL NEED: pencil, paper, computer, Internet connection.

Carry out some research into the history of tobacco using information books and the Internet. How did it arrive in this country and who was the first person to bring it in?

FURTHER IDEAS:

- Investigate the dangers of smoking and what it can do to your lungs. (S)

- Find out some facts and figures about death from smoking. Produce some charts to show your results. (M)

- Make a list of the side effects of smoking on **a.** A smoker **b.** Someone living with a heavy smoker. (E)

- Write a story about how someone smoking causes a terrible accident. (E)

- Make up a short play about someone who becomes part of a gang and then is introduced to smoking but refuses to join in. (E)

HEALTH EDUCATION

SAYING NO TO SMOKING

PURPOSE: To discuss how you can say no to those who want you to join in and smoke.

TEACHER INFORMATION:

Most children who smoke readily admit that they don't like doing it and only take part because it makes them feel grown up. Other children say they do not want to say no because if someone offers them a cigarette it looks soft.

There are a number of factors that need to influence their decision not to smoke:

HEALTH REASONS: Smoking can do a lot of damage to you and cause premature death.
SMELL: It can get in your hair, breath, clothes and in the house.
COST: 20 cigarettes can cost more than £4.00 a packet, if you smoke one packet a day that is over £28.00 a week!
FIRE RISK: Hundreds of people every year are killed by fires caused by cigarettes.
RISK TO OTHERS: i.e. passive smoking. People can become ill and die because of others in their family who smoke.
STAINS: It can cause yellow stains on your fingers and on your teeth.

There are plenty of myths about smoking. These include:

- It looks cool and grown up
- It calms your nerves
- It keeps your weight down
- Smoking gives you confidence

Discuss these myths with the class.

KEY ACTIVITY (M)
YOU WILL NEED: pencil, paper.

Carry out a survey with friends and family and find out how many smoke and how many a day. Produce a graph or chart based on your findings. Use this chart to start a discussion in groups on the dangers of smoking. Get the others in the class to decide whether or not it is a good idea to smoke. At the end of your discussion see how many people have voted for smoking and how many against.

If members of the class have family who smoke ask them why?

FURTHER IDEAS:
- Make up a rhyme or advert to encourage people to stop smoking. (E,Ms)
- Invite a nurse or doctor in to talk about the dangers. (S)
- Find out which shops and public places in your area ban smoking. (E)
- Ask several members of the class to say what might happen to them if they were caught smoking at home. (E)

HEALTH EDUCATION

ALCOHOL - THE FACTS

PURPOSE: To explain the facts about Alcohol.

TEACHER INFORMATION:

Alcohol is brewed or distilled from a variety of things including grapes, cereals and vegetables. It can be flavoured with herbs. If drunk in large quantities it can seriously harm your body.

Alcohol comes in three main types:
- **BEER**
- **WINE**
- **SPIRITS**

It is available in a wide range of outlets, pubs, supermarkets and can often be found in the home.

There are some forms of alcohol which cannot be drunk. These include shoe polish, window cleaning creams, de-icing sprays and solvents.

Like smoking, alcohol is said to relieve stress and make you happier. This may be true in small amounts but drinking a lot of alcohol can be extremely dangerous.

Alcohol has a different effect on different people. The more you drink the greater the effect.

KEY ACTIVITY (M)
YOU WILL NEED: pencil, paper.

Carry out a survey amongst adults and children as to their favourite cold drink. Use the results to have a class discussion on whether alcohol is popular or not. It is important that the teacher does not impose their own value judgements on the group.

Make a list of the most popular alcoholic drink amongst adults you know.

FURTHER IDEAS:

- Discuss why adults will not let children drink alcohol when they may well drink it themselves. (E)
- Find out something about the history of beer. When was it first introduced into this country. (H)
- Make up some non-alcoholic cocktails e.g. lemonade and orange juice. Which are the favourites? (S)
- Carry out a survey on the different types of containers used for non-alcoholic drinks. (M)

THE DANGERS OF ALCOHOL

PURPOSE: To look at the various dangers of alcohol.

TEACHER INFORMATION:

Over 1,000 children under the age of 15 are taken into hospital every year due to alcohol poisoning.

Alcohol can do a great deal of damage to your body. It can harm your liver and also make you sick and even cause unconsciousness.

The law says:
- When you are 14 you can go into a bar with an adult but you cannot buy anything.
- When you are 16 you can drink some types of alcohol but only with a meal.
- If you are 18 you can buy alcohol on your own.

Alcohol can kill brain cells and irritate the lining of the stomach. If someone drinks over a long period of time it may cause liver disease or make heart disease more likely.

Drinking alcohol and driving is extremely dangerous and can kill. Even small amounts of alcohol can slow down your senses. Never let anyone who has been drinking drive. They could kill you, themselves and innocent people. It is very dangerous.

Alcohol can also lead to public disorder, fights and hooliganism which can break out at football matches or where there are a few people gathered together.

Alcohol is measured in units. A safe limit for a man is 21 units a week and for a woman 14 units a week. It takes the liver one hour to process one unit.

- **A small glass of wine is one unit**
- **Half a pint of lager is one unit**
- **A single whisky is one unit**
- **Half a pint of strong lager is two units**

Alcohol reaches the brain within five minutes of being swallowed. It slows down the activity in your brain. It affects women more quickly than men. Nearly 90% of boys in England have drunk alcohol by the time they are 13.

Some people do not drink because:
- Of their religion
- They don't like it
- Because they have an alcohol problem.
- Of their work
- Of medical reasons

KEY ACTIVITY (M)

YOU WILL NEED: pencil, paper.

How many units did each of these people drink in a week?
Jake had 5 pints of lager.
Sue had 7 large glasses of wine.
Bob had 3 small glasses of whisky, 7 pints of strong lager and 4 small glasses of wine.
Tina had 6 small glasses of whisky and 5 pints of lager.

Was anyone over their recommended limit for the week?

FURTHER IDEAS:
- Find out how a breathalyser works. (S)
- Make a series of drawings of pub signs. See if you can find out what they mean? (A)
- Design a poster giving alternatives to drinking alcohol that might make you happy. (A)
- Carry out a family survey and ask them how often they drink alcohol, where they drink it, when they started drinking, how much they drink a week? Use your results to construct some charts. (M)

HEALTH EDUCATION

DRUGS THAT HELP

PURPOSE: To look at a range of drugs that help us.

TEACHER INFORMATION:

The purpose of the following two pages is to provide children with the information so that they can differentiate between legal and illegal drugs, and to make their own decisions in a non judgmental environment.

Drugs are chemical substances that affect your body or your mind.

Both tobacco and alcohol are drugs. All medicines are drugs but not all drugs are medicines.

When you are ill, the doctor will give you medicine to take which will make you better. It is OK as long as you follow the instructions and they have been given to you by a sensible person in authority such as a doctor or your parents. Often drugs like this come with special instructions and also special lids to stop young children opening them up.

There are a large number of legal drugs that you can buy. These include cough medicine, pain killers and antibiotics. Caffeine that is found in tea and coffee is a drug and so is nicotine and alcohol.

Many legal drugs are used to make people better but you should remember that even legal drugs can be dangerous.

KEY ACTIVITY (S)
YOU WILL NEED: pencil, paper.

Make a list of drugs that can help you. Write down where you can buy them and what they are used for.

FURTHER IDEAS:

- Write a short story involving a doctor, an ambulance and a hospital. (E)

- Find out what these people did for medicine: Florence Nightingale, Marie Curie, Edward Jenner and Louis Pasteur. (H)

- Draw a map showing where you can buy medicines in your local area. (G,M)

HEALTH EDUCATION

DRUG ABUSE

PURPOSE: To consider drugs that are dangerous to us.

TEACHER INFORMATION:

There are a number of drugs that are not legal and are very dangerous. These include cocaine and heroin.

Taking these drugs can be very dangerous and people can become addicted to them. That means they cannot get through the day without them. To get the drug they need money and often they will have to steal to pay for the drug. Sometimes they lose their job and even their home. The longer they stay addicted to the drug the worse it is for their health. It can kill them.

There is no guarantee as to what these drugs contain.

Drugs can alter the way you think and act.

If you are found in possession of drugs or using them you could be in serious trouble.

You should never pick up a syringe as it could be very dangerous.

You may be able to spot if someone is on drugs if:

- Their speech is slurred
- Unusual eye movements
- Odd speech
- Mood swings
- Drowsiness

KEY ACTIVITY (M)

YOU WILL NEED: pencil, large piece of paper.

Draw a map of the area and mark in areas where you think you might be at risk from being approached by undesirable individuals or groups.

FURTHER IDEAS:

- Ask someone from the local social services or police to come in and talk about the dangers of drugs. (E)
- Make up a play about someone who is persuaded to take drugs. What happens to them? Now act out a play where the person says no to drugs. (E)
- Draw a poster warning people about taking drugs. (A)
- Which of these drugs would be dangerous to take and why? Coffee, cigarettes, weed killer, glue, hairspray, whisky. Discuss. (E)

HEALTH EDUCATION

KEY LINKS

MATHEMATICS:	Dangers Of Alcohol
	Drug Abuse
	Alcohol - The Facts
	Saying No To Smoking
	Drugs That Help

ENGLISH:	Smoking - The Facts
	Alcohol - The Facts
	Saying No To Smoking
	Dangers Of Alcohol
	Drug Abuse

SCIENCE:	Smoking - The Facts
	Drugs That Help
	Saying No To Smoking
	Saying No To Alcohol
	Dangers Of Alcohol

HISTORY:	Smoking - The facts
	Alcohol - The Facts
	Drugs That Help

MUSIC:	Saying No To Smoking

ART & DESIGN:	Dangers Of Alcohol
	Drug Abuse

ICT:	Smoking - The Facts

HEALTH EDUCATION

FIRST AID

PURPOSE:
- **To make children aware of the importance of first aid in their own locality.**
- **To help build up a wider knowledge of these issues in the immediate area and further afield.**
- **To encourage individual thinking and decision making.**

FACT: The Red Cross was started more than 135 years ago by Henri Dunant, a Swiss businessman. There is a Red Cross Museum in Geneva, Switzerland.

FACT: We can only survive for 5 minutes without oxygen.

Page 59	**WHAT TO DO IN AN EMERGENCY**
Page 60	**SAVING LIVES**
Page 61	**RECOVERY FACTS**
Page 62	**SHOCK AND TREATMENT**
Page 63	**A BASIC FIRST AID KIT**
Page 64	**SIMPLE FIRST AID**
Page 65	**KEY LINKS CHART**

TEACHER'S NOTE:
RESOURCES FOR FIRST AID INCLUDE:
- The Early Years First Aid Handbook (5-7 years)
- The First Aid Handbook (7-11 years)
- Junior Medics (7-11 years)
- Play Safe, Stay Safe, Keep Safe (7-11 years)
- Junior Citizen Handbook (7-11 years)

WHAT TO DO IN AN EMERGENCY

PURPOSE: To understand how to cope in an emergency.

TEACHER INFORMATION:
What happens in the first few minutes of an emergency can be a matter of life or death. It is important, therefore, that children have at least a basic understanding of how to cope.

If they suspect someone is injured they should keep very calm and make sure that the person who has been injured is safe.

BASIC RULES:
1. They should keep safe and not risk injury themselves.
2. They should try and find out what happened to the person. If needed they should carry out the ABC plan. Check the AIRWAY. Tilt the head and lift the chin up.
Make sure they are BREATHING for up to ten seconds. Make sure that their chest is moving. They should check the person's breath on their cheek. If they are not breathing then they should start mouth to mouth ventilations. Check the CIRCULATION. Look for movement and see if they are breathing or swallowing.
3. They should give help if they can but only move the person if they need to put them in the recovery position.
4. They should not give the injured person anything to drink or eat.
5. Once the person has been made comfortable go and get help as quickly as possible.

IN AN EMERGENCY IT IS VITAL TO:
- Stop
- Think
- Look for any dangers
- Get help as quickly as possible
- Give help
- Keep yourself safe

KEY ACTIVITY (S,M)
YOU WILL NEED: pencil, paper.
Take your pulse when you are lying down. Then get up and walk around for two minutes, take it again. Record any differences. Try the same test but this time run rather than walk. Does your pulse rate increase or decrease after you have finished running for two minutes. Why is this? What do you think is happening inside your body? Carry out some tests with other children in your class.

WARNING: This activity should not be carried out with children who might suffer from asthma or chest problems.

FURTHER IDEAS:
- Write a story about an emergency. What happened? It could be written as a letter to someone or as a news report. (E)
- Search the Internet for information on a local ambulance service, the Red Cross or the St John Ambulance Service. (ICT)
- Ask a member of the emergency services to come and explain what you should do if you are faced with an emergency. (E)
- Explain to the class what the emergency ABC plan is. (E)

FIRST AID

SAVING LIVES

PURPOSE: To find out more about the ambulance service and what it does.

TEACHER INFORMATION:

When you dial 999 one of the services you may ask for is an ambulance. Once they receive a call they respond by sending out highly trained medics who are trained to save lives.

Ambulances are located all over the country. In Scotland the service started in 1775 with the introduction in Edinburgh of two sedan chairs that were used to move sick people about.

If a paramedic arrives on the scene they may carry a wide range of special equipment. Ambulances are equipped to deal with a variety of emergencies. They carry stretchers, collars, splints, blood monitors, defibrillators and a range of bandages.

The Ambulance Service receive more than 4 million calls a year.

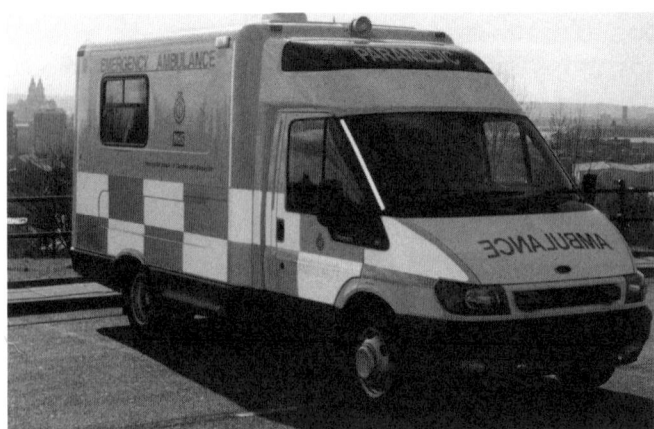

A typical ambulance.

An emergency scene.

KEY ACTIVITY (E)
YOU WILL NEED: pencil, paper.

Imagine that you are a paramedic. Describe, using a cartoon format, a day in your life. The cartoon should include a simple storyline underneath each picture.

FURTHER IDEAS:
- Design and paint a large poster to be used by the ambulance service for recruiting new staff. (DT, A)
- Make up a play about an emergency that is attended by an ambulance crew. (E)
- Find out what you can about the blood system in the human body. Draw a diagram showing where your heart is and how your blood is pumped round your body. (S)
- *Arrange to make a visit to your local ambulance station or get one of their officers to come in and talk about their job. (E)
- *If there are any parents who are nurses, midwives or doctors get them to come in and explain what they do. (E)
- Using the Internet find out about the Flying Doctor Ambulance Service in Australia. Also investigate air ambulances in this country. (ICT)

FIRST AID

RECOVERY FACTS

PURPOSE: To explain the recovery position and mouth to mouth ventilation.

TEACHER INFORMATION:
These are two life saving activities that can be taught.

Recovery position

- If someone is unconscious then they may die if their airway gets blocked so they must be put into the recovery position as quickly as possible.

- The person should be laid on their back and if they wear glasses these should be taken off. Any tight clothing should be loosened. Kneel beside them and tilt their head backwards and lift up their chin.

- Their legs should be straightened and their arm next to you should be bent at right angles. Their other arm should be brought across their body and you should hold their hand against their cheek.

- Keeping their hand against their cheek take hold of the leg that is furthermost away from you and pull their knee up. Their foot must be on the floor. Holding the person's hand up against their cheek, pull gently on their leg and roll them towards you. If possible do not leave them on their own and keep them warm. However if you do have to go and make a 999 call when you get back be sure to check their breathing.

- Remember blood can be infected so don't touch areas of blood more than necessary. If you can, cover your hands with plastic bags or gloves and wash them thoroughly afterwards.

Mouth to Mouth
- Put the person onto their back. Make sure nothing is blocking the airways.
- Tilt their head backwards.
- Pinch their nose tightly.
- Take a long breath, seal your lips with theirs. Blow into their mouth and wait for their chest to rise.
- Stop and take your head away. See if the person's chest falls as they start to breathe out.
- Keep going until they begin breathing themselves.
- Never practice this on someone who is breathing properly.

KEY ACTIVITY (H)
YOU WILL NEED: pencil, paper.

Investigate what life was like one hundred years ago. Then write a short story based on either an emergency on a train 100 years ago or in a street. What would happen? Would it be different from today, and if so how?

FURTHER IDEAS:
- Draw a map of the country then draw some pictures of different types of accidents e.g. motorway, rural, at sea, on mountains. Mark on the map where these kind of accidents might happen. (G,A)
- Collect together a range of material on different accidents that have happened locally. In how many cases were the emergency services required? (G,E)
- Get someone from your local ambulance service to come in and demonstrate the recovery position and mouth to mouth ventilation. (E)
- Find out what kind of accidents most commonly happen in the home, at school in the work place. Produce a graph showing your results. (M)
- *What kind of accidents might cause someone to fall over and hurt themselves? Discuss (E).

FIRST AID

SHOCK AND TREATMENT

PURPOSE: To explain the treatment of shock.

TEACHER INFORMATION:

If someone has lost a lot of blood or they have suffered a great deal of pain they may go into a state of shock.

You can spot this by looking at the person and seeing if:
1. They feel weak and faint.
2. Their skin is pale, cold and feels damp.
3. They are starting to feel sick.
4. Their breathing is very fast and shallow.

If this happens then you should carry out the following:
1. Lay them down making sure that their head is kept low.
2. Raise their legs and loosen tight clothing.
3. Keep the person warm.
4. Dial 999 for an ambulance.

It is very important that you help as quickly as possible.

If someone has suffered an **ELECTRIC SHOCK**, then it is important that you do not touch them. If you do then you may suffer a similar shock as electricity can pass from one person to another.

If you can, switch off the electricity at the meter box and pull out any plug.

If you cannot turn off the power you should stand on a dry block of wood or paper and use a dry wooden pole to try and move the person away from the electrical source. Do not touch this source!

Dial 999 as soon as possible.

REMEMBER:
- Electrical current can also cause electrical burns.
- It can travel through the air, poles, and water to get to you.
- Never go near electrical sub-stations.
- Never play with kites near power lines.

KEY ACTIVITY (E)

YOU WILL NEED: pencil, crayons or paints, paper.

Make a list of the kind of situations that could lead to someone suffering from shock. Then create your own poster pointing out what people should do if someone is suffering from shock after a large loss of blood or accident.

FURTHER IDEAS:
- Organise an assembly to show what can be done if someone is suffering from shock. (E)
- Write to the local power supply company and ask them to send a selection of material on electrical safety. (E)
- Draw a map of your area and mark in any high voltage power lines or cables. (M)
- Write a story for younger children which stresses the importance of keeping away from electricity. (E)
- Why can kite flying or fishing sometimes be dangerous when there are pylons or overhead electrical cables about? Discuss. (E)
- Get a local nurse to come in and talk about what to do when a person goes into shock. (E)

FIRST AID

A BASIC FIRST AID KIT

PURPOSE: To discuss and decide what should go into a basic first aid kit.

TEACHER INFORMATION:
Discuss why it is important for places to have their own first aid kits.
- What kind of buildings need them e.g. offices, schools, workplaces? Where should they be located?
- Should anyone be trained to use them?
- When should they be used?
- Should homes be equipped with a first aid kit? What should be in it?
- Should public vehicles have them? e.g. buses, trains. Who should be able to use them?
- Are they fitted to cars as standard equipment? If not why not?

Here are some suggested items that could be put into a First Aid Kit:
- Cotton wool
- Safety pins
- Different types of bandages
- Plasters of different sizes
- Scissors
- Clinical thermometer
- Plastic disposable gloves
- Sterile dressings

Discuss why each of these items would be useful and what else might be included. Make a list of minor accidents and what could be used from the kit.

KEY ACTIVITY (DT)
YOU WILL NEED: pencil, crayons or paints, card, glue, scissors.

Design and create a basic first aid kit. What kind of box would you need, how big, would it have to be protected? Decide what should go in it and then make a mock up of the box and its contents. It is important that you decide on who it is for and how it is to be used.

FURTHER IDEAS:
- Write to some car manufacturers and ask if they have first aid kits fitted in their new vehicles. (E)
- Who is in charge of first aid in the school? Where is the first aid kit kept? When is it used? Carry out a survey to find when the first aid kit is most heavily used. Produce some charts to show your results. (E,M)
- Carry out some experiments on temperature using a thermometer. (S)
- Investigate the history of plasters and antiseptic cream. Use the Internet for your investigations or maybe write to the manufacturers. (S,ICT,E)
- Get someone to come in and explain what makes a good first aid kit. (E)
- Make up a holiday first aid kit for the following types of holidays: skiing, safari, beach, horse riding. (DT)

FIRST AID

SIMPLE FIRST AID

PURPOSE: To explain some simple first aid procedures which could be used in an emergency.

TEACHER INFORMATION:
Remember that if someone has an accident it is important to keep calm, make sure that no one is in danger.

Some simple First Aid:

- **A CUT:** First wash your hands in warm soapy water. If the cut is dirty wash it under a cold tap. Carefully pat the wound with a clean tissue until it is dry. Keep the wound covered and then clean around it. Pat it dry and then stick a plaster on it. If the cut is deep use a clean pad and seek help.

- **A BRUISE:** Cool the bruise using something very cold such as an ice pack. Do this for around 10 minutes, it should help the swelling go down. Seek help if it is a bad bruise.

- **NOSE BLEEDS:** Sit the person down and bend their head forward to stop any blood being swallowed. Get them to hold their nose tightly and breathe through the mouth. They should not cough or sniff as this may cause clotting. If their nose is still bleeding after half an hour you need to get medical help. Remember to wear plastic gloves if you are dealing with blood and wash your hands afterwards.

- **BROKEN OR FRACTURED LIMBS:** Do not move the person and seek immediate help. In the case of an open fracture they should be supported and any open wound covered.

- **SPRAINED LIMBS:** Try to rest the limb, put an ice pack on it, put a compress on it and bandage the sprain. Then raise the damaged limb so that it is elevated. Remember if you don't know what to do, keep calm and get immediate help.

- **OTHER TIPS:** If someone is choking bend their head over their chest, slap them on the back between their shoulder blades at least five times with the flat of your hand. Repeat this until the blockage is cleared. If you can't do this seek help at once. If someone is suffering from sunburn ask them to sip cold water or run cold water over the affected area. Some forms of aftersun lotion may help. If their skin is blistering get help.

KEY ACTIVITY (M)
YOU WILL NEED: pencil, paper.

Carry out a survey on your class to find out how many people have suffered from minor accidents in the past month. Use the information to create a series of charts showing the most common accidents. Carry out a similar survey in adults, either at school or in your family. Is there any difference in adult and child related accidents.

FURTHER IDEAS:
- Find out what methods our body uses to repair itself. (S)
- Make a list of minor accidents that might happen in these places: on a pleasure boat; on a railway station; at a cafe; on a bus; on a windy hill; in a supermarket. (E,G)
- What kind of minor accidents could happen to a young child: in the kitchen; in the bathroom; in the living room; in the garden. How could they be dealt with? (E,S)
- Draw a plan of your home or school, mark in any places where you think minor accidents could happen. (M)

FIRST AID

KEY LINKS

MATHEMATICS: What To Do In An Emergency
Recovery Facts
Shock And Treatment
A Basic First Aid Kit
Simple First Aid

ENGLISH: What To Do In An Emergency
Saving Lives
Recovery Facts Shock And Treatment
A Basic First Aid Kit
Simple First Aid

SCIENCE: What To Do In An Emergency
Saving Lives
A Basic First Aid Kit
Simple First Aid

HISTORY: Recovery Facts

GEOGRAPHY: Recovery Facts
Simple First Aid

DESIGN AND TECHNOLOGY: Saving Lives

MUSIC:

ART & DESIGN: Saving Lives
Recovery Facts

ICT: What To Do In An Emergency
Saving Lives
A Basic First Aid Kit

FIRST AID

CITIZENSHIP AND COMMUNITY RESPONSIBILITY

PURPOSE:
- **To develop an awareness of citizenship and community responsibility.**
- **To help build up a wider knowledge of these issues in the immediate area and further afield.**
- **To encourage individual thinking and decision making.**

FACT: There are nearly half a million people without homes in the United Kingdom.

FACT: There are over three and three quarter million people living in the European Union at the present.

Page 67 **SAFETY IN NUMBERS**

Page 68 **FRIENDSHIP**

Page 69 **SIMILARITIES AND DIFFERENCES**

Page 70 **MAKING DECISIONS**

Page 71 **PART OF THE COMMUNITY**

Page 72 **COMMUNITY GROUPS**

Page 73 **KEY LINKS CHART**

TEACHER'S NOTE:
RESOURCES FOR CITIZENSHIP & COMMUNITY RESPONSIBILITY INCLUDE:
- Will Power's Early Years Book of Choices (5-7 years)
- Will Power's Beware (7-11 years)
- Junior Citizen Handbook (7-11 years)
- Play Safe, Stay Safe, Keep Safe (7-11 years)
- The Young Persons Guide To Bullying (7-11 years)

SAFETY IN NUMBERS

PURPOSE: To consider the importance of living as a community and looking after each other.

TEACHER INFORMATION:

It is important that young people realise the importance of life as a community and that for us to live safely and happily, we need to take responsibility and live by certain rules.

Living in groups means that we have to learn to co-operate with other people and interact with each other. We live in a multi-cultural society and, therefore, it is often important that we sometimes think of the good of the community rather than the individual. Family life is a vital part of our culture and society and so it is important that children develop a sense of responsibility to others rather than just themselves.

Each person can play a part in their family by helping out and taking on a role, whether it be looking after others in the family, or helping with the shopping. As children get older they need to understand that they will take on more and more roles as they become more and more part of the community and society generally.

It should be remembered that most of us come from some sort of mixed background including French, Celtic, Flemish, Anglo Saxon, Viking, Indian, Caribbean, or African.

Staying safe is one part of this and caring for those who cannot care for themselves should be one of our responsibilities. This means looking after the old and the very young.

We can help by avoiding street crime and informing our neighbours about possible bogus callers. We could make regular visits to the sick and elderly in the area and seek ways to help them. If we see a young child lost or in distress then we should help them.

KEY ACTIVITY (E,G)

YOU WILL NEED: pencil, paper.

Find out what is being done in your area to:
- Reduce street crime
- Stop joyriding
- Increase personal safety
- Improve security in people's homes
- Stop bogus callers.

Produce a booklet on ways in which your community is helping to improve the area.

FURTHER IDEAS:

- Think of some ways in which you could bring people in your community closer together. (E)
- Write a letter to a friend or relative abroad, tell them what life is like in your community and what you are doing to help each other. Get them to write back and let you know what they are doing. (G,E)
- Examine the way other creatures live together in a group. These could include insects or mammals such as lions or elephants. (S)
- Play some games in PE where children have to work as a group rather than as an individual. (PE)
- What is happening at present in the local community that involves people working together. Are there any projects? Find out what you can about them and see if there is any way you can get involved. (E)

CITIZENSHIP & COMMUNITY RESPONSIBILITY

FRIENDSHIP

PURPOSE: To consider how important it is to have friends.

TEACHER INFORMATION:

We all make friends as we grow up. Some of these are short term and other long term. They are often people we can rely on or go to if we need help.

If you have a friend then it is important that you trust each other. Here are some simple statements about friends that could be discussed with a group or the class.

- Friends should keep secrets.
- You should wait until a friend offers a secret and not pry.
- Friends should share both happy and sad times.
- You should stand up for a friend.
- You should support a friend.
- You can ask a friend for support.
- Offer help to a friend, do not wait for it to be asked for.
- Always return borrowed things.
- If a friend hurts your feelings say so, do not sulk or turn your back on them.
- Look into your friends eyes when you talk to them.
- Don't joke or tease a friend.
- Don't be jealous of friend's other relationships.

Get the children to add other things to the list and come up with the three most important rules. Do they agree with all of them?

KEY ACTIVITY (H,E)
YOU WILL NEED: pencil, paper.

Investigate some famous friendships e.g. Sherlock Holmes and Doctor Watson, The Three Musketeers, Ratty and Mole in Wind in the Willows, Winnie the Pooh and Christopher Robin, Batman and Robin, Del Boy and Rodney. Why did they get on well together?

Make up a book of famous friends fictional or real.

FURTHER IDEAS:

- Draw some pictures of friends together. (A)
- Write a story about two friends who help each other out. (E)
- Set up some activities where the children work in pairs. After they have finished get them to discuss what it was like working with someone else rather than on their own. (E)
- Discuss why it is important to have friends. (E)

CITIZENSHIP & COMMUNITY RESPONSIBILITY

SIMILARITIES AND DIFFERENCES

PURPOSE: To look at the similarities and differences in cultures and begin to understand that others may have different ideas and customs to ourselves.

TEACHER INFORMATION:

There is a mix of different cultures and ethnic groups in this country. It is, therefore, very important that children realise that respect breeds respect and if they learn to understand other people's customs and ways they will gain more respect themselves.

Over half the ethnic population of the UK were born here. Young children easily mix with each other and often have lots in common. They enjoy the same sport, music and food and in many areas they do not let issues come between them.

There are a number of different religions practiced in this country and it would be a good idea to investigate some of the major festivals:

Easter, Christmas - Christian
Passover, Hannukah - Judaism
Festival of Balasaki, Birthday of Guru - Sikhism

Holi, Diwali - Hindu
Ramadan - Islam
Buddhism - Buddha's birth, life and death.

The main religions followed in the UK are Christianity, Islam, Hinduism, Buddhism, Sikhism and Judaism.

Christians believe in Jesus Christ as the Son of God whilst Moslems follow the Koran and believe in Allah. Hindus worship many gods whilst Buddhists believe in the teaching of Buddha and the sacredness of life. Sikhism is based on the teaching of ten Sikh spiritual leaders whilst Judaism is the oldest living religion and believe in one god as chronicled in the Hebrew Bible.

Followers: (approximately)
Christians - 2,000 million
Hindus - 800 million
Sikhs - 15 million

Muslims - 1,000 million +
Buddhists - 350 million
Jews - 15 million

KEY ACTIVITY (E,G,RE)
YOU WILL NEED: pencil, paper, colours.

Investigate a major festival that is about to come up. Find out as much as you can about it. Ask a parent who is about to celebrate it to come in and explain it to the class. Decorate the classroom accordingly.

FURTHER IDEAS:
- Write a poem or story based on a religious festival you have attended. (E)
- Investigate the different ways people are baptised, married, or buried in different religions. (E,G)
- Find a story from a major religion and turn it into a play which could become part of an assembly. (E)
- Find out which religions are worshiped in your area. (G)
- Ask representatives from several faiths to come in and talk to the children about their traditions and customs. (E)
- Investigate the importance of numbers and religion. (M)
- Research some of the different calendars used by different faiths. (M)
- Play some games linked to different religions. Get the children to suggest some they might play at home. (PE)

CITIZENSHIP & COMMUNITY RESPONSIBILITY

MAKING DECISIONS

PURPOSE: To look at how one can make an informed decision.

TEACHER INFORMATION:

As children grow up they need to make more and more decisions for themselves. This might include not agreeing with the rest of a gang or their friends. Everyone is different and lots of different people and things will influence their decisions.

These will include:

parents or carers
teachers
newspapers and magazines
friends

brothers and sisters
television and radio
adverts
themselves

Often they will have to make decisions when they are on their own. They must realise they should not be influenced by others who may have an ulterior motive for their actions. This might be to get them to start smoking, accept drugs or take part in bullying. It is at times like these when they will need to be strong and have willpower.

Remember if someone is trying to get them to do or say something, it is totally up to the individual to make the decision. There may also be times when they will need to persuade others to make decisions to stop stealing or getting into trouble. At times like this they should understand that some techniques are unlikely to work.

These include:
- Sarcasm
- Accusations
- Threats
- Embarrassment
- Infallibility e.g. because I say so!

If they are trying to get someone to change their mind then they need to:
- Stay calm.
- Listen to what they have to say.
- Praise the other person's good points.
- Be supportive.
- Explain why they shouldn't do something wrong.

There may be times when the situation is dangerous and a decision has to be made quickly, but also safely. Talk about what kind of things go through your mind if you are in this type of situation e.g. needing to stay calm, think clearly, asking for help, acting quickly.

KEY ACTIVITY (E)

YOU WILL NEED: pencil, paper.

Organise a role play exercise in which:
a. A child has to make a decision either to go into a shop and steal something with their friends or walk away.
b. Persuade a friend that they should stop smoking or bullying someone.

FURTHER IDEAS:
- Discuss how children might get respect from their peers and adults. (E)
- Make a list of people who have had to make very important decisions in history. (H)
- Design a poster based on making decisions. (DT)
- Talk about daily decisions e.g. what to eat, which route to take to school. (E)

PART OF THE COMMUNITY

PURPOSE: To look at ways in which we can become more part of the community.

TEACHER INFORMATION:

Living together we are part of a community. As a member of a community it is important that we take responsibility for what we do as our actions can have a great influence on those around us.

If we do not respect the community we live in because of our selfishness, or lack of social responsibility, it may cause things to deteriorate.

There are many ways in which we can help improve the community. These include:

- Showing respect for others.
- Being responsible for ourselves and our pets.
- Setting an example to younger children.
- Helping out.
- Being polite and considerate on public transport.
- Helping others.
- Caring for our environment.
- Respecting property.
- Supporting people.
- Considering other people's feelings and needs.
- Treating people as equals.
- Being honest.

KEY ACTIVITY (G, E)

YOU WILL NEED: pencil, colours, large piece of paper.

Investigate ways in which the local environment could be improved, e.g. new play areas, better security, more litter bins. Draw a plan and mark in your improvements. You might also like to write to the authorities and make some suggestions on a range of improvements to make where you live a better place.

FURTHER IDEAS:

- Find out how we can make a difference in:
  a. Countries where there is a shortage of food.
  b. Countries which have suffered from a natural disaster e.g. flood or erupting volcano.
  c. In cities where there are a large number of homeless people. (G)
- Look at differences in mathematics e.g. one and one thousand, one gram and a kilogram, one centimetre and one metre. Make a chart showing these differences. (M)
- Ask someone from a community organisation that helps people who are in distress to visit your school. (E)
- Make up a play or dance about being part of a community. (Ms)
- Organise a class event in which everybody takes part. (E)

CITIZENSHIP & COMMUNITY RESPONSIBILITY

COMMUNITY GROUPS

PURPOSE: To understand the importance of community groups and how to take part in these.

TEACHER INFORMATION:

Communities are made of lots of different individuals and groups. Some of these groups will be able to help and support the individual, family or group.

Within your own community there may be social clubs, sports clubs and church groups. These all work together to make for a richer and more productive community.

Outside our immediate community there are larger organisations that have been set up to help people generally. Some of these are run by councils or the Government whilst others are charities.

Many of these nationally recognised charities provide services that can help people when they are in need.

THESE INCLUDE:

CHILDLINE: Free phoneline for children who need help. All the information is confidential.

KIDSCAPE: Another charity that helps children in need.

NSPCC: A long established charity that is concerned with cruelty to children.

SAMARITANS: A free phoneline that helps people who are desperate. They are there to listen.

SHELTER: An organisation that has been set up to help the homeless and those who sleep on the streets.

KEY ACTIVITY (H,ICT)

YOU WILL NEED: paper, pencil, computer.

Find out the history and background of one main charity that helps people in need. You may be able to get the information from the Internet or by writing to the organisation concerned. Put up a display of your work and invite someone from the organisation in to talk about what they do.

FURTHER IDEAS:

- Get one of the leaders of a local club to come in and talk about what they do. (E)
- Design a poster for one of the local community groups. (A)
- Pretend to hold the first meeting of a new help group in the area. Divide into those at the front and those in the audience. What kind of questions do you think would be asked? (E)
- Act out a story based around someone stopping and helping someone else. There are many examples in different religions of these types of stories. You may like to choose one of these. (E)
- Make an investigation of mammals that live together underground e.g. rabbits. What kind of community have they developed. (S)

KEY LINKS

MATHEMATICS: Similarities And Differences
Part Of The Community

ENGLISH: Safety In Numbers
Friendship
Similarities And Differences
Making Decisions
Part Of The Community
Community Groups

SCIENCE: Safety In Numbers
Community Groups

HISTORY: Friendship
Making Decisions
Community Groups

GEOGRAPHY: Safety In Numbers
Similarities And Differences
Part Of The Community

DESIGN AND TECHNOLOGY: Making Decisions

MUSIC: Part Of The Community

ART & DESIGN: Friendship
Community Groups

PE: Safety In Numbers

ICT: Community Groups

RE: Similarities And Differences

CITIZENSHIP & COMMUNITY RESPONSIBILITY

THE LAW AND YOUNG PEOPLE

PURPOSE:
- **To develop a better understanding of the law.**
- **To help build up a wider understanding of these matters within their own experiences and to extend this into the outside world.**
- **To encourage individual thinking and decision making.**

FACT: Crime costs the shopkeepers of this country around £2 billion a year.

FACT: Once you have been the victim of a crime there is a one in three chance that you will be a victim again.

Page 75	**WHAT IS THE LAW?**
Page 76	**SAYING NO**
Page 77	**CAR CRIME**
Page 78	**ALCOHOL, DRUGS, SOLVENT ABUSE AND THE LAW**
Page 79	**TRESPASS AND VANDALISM**
Page 80	**SHOPLIFTING AND OTHER FORMS OF THEFT**
Page 81	**KEY LINKS CHART**

TEACHER'S NOTE:
RESOURCES FOR THE LAW AND YOUNG PEOPLE INCLUDE:
- Will Power's Beware (7-11 years)
- Junior Citizen Handbook (7-11 years)
- Play Safe, Stay Safe, Keep Safe (7-11 years)
- Respect Your Life Your Choice (11-14 years)

WHAT IS THE LAW?

PURPOSE: To explain why we have rules and laws.

TEACHER INFORMATION:

Rules and laws are there so that society can live in harmony with each other. Without these rules life would be extremely difficult. It is thought that the first laws, as we understand them today, were introduced around 1700 BC.

Laws in this country are made by Parliament. There are three sections to our Parliament:
- The House of Commons
- The House of Lords
- The Queen

Laws are made in Parliament and have to be signed by the Queen before they are considered law.

The House of Commons is full of our representatives so we do in fact have some degree of say in the creation of these laws.

There are a variety of different laws. These include:

- **CRIMINAL:** If anyone breaks the law e.g steals something from a shop, they are prosecuted for their crime. If a police officer sees someone breaking a law, it is their job to arrest them, if they have reasonable suspicion that an offence has or is to be committed. It needs, however, to be made clear that a police officer does not have the power to punish the criminal. This has to be done through a court of law.

- **CIVIL:** Civil laws are usually those that have been created to help sort out people's disputes and trade e.g. ownership of boundaries, house buying.

- **MORAL:** These are laws that come from a sense of right and wrong. There are a large number of religious laws which exist.

If a serious crime is committed then the case is dealt with either by a magistrate, justice of the peace or in more serious cases a judge and jury. The jury consists of 12 men and women in England and Wales and 16 in Scotland. The job of the jury is to listen to the evidence and then make a decision on whether the accused is guilty or not.

If someone is found guilty of an offence they may either go to prison, be fined, or given community service.

KEY ACTIVITY (E)

YOU WILL NEED: paper, pencil.

Make a list of ten rules that you think all people in the world should follow. Consider some of the rules found in different religions.

Write out these rules on a large piece of paper. Now make a list of ten rules which could be used in your classroom. Are any of the rules similar to your 'world list'? What should happen to people who break the rules?

FURTHER IDEAS:

- Write a newspaper report based on the arrest of an innocent suspect. (E)
- Recreate a courtroom event. Select a jury of twelve, decide on who will be the judge, the defendant, the prosecutor and the defence. Decide on the crime. This could be something taken from a story book e.g. the stealing of the Quidditch rules from Hogwarts or the disappearance of certain items from the Queen Vic or the Rovers Return. Try to bring some humour into it. (E)
- Find out what might have happened to someone if they had stolen a small item say 500 years ago, 200 years ago, today. Has the punishment changed and if so why? (H)
- Make up a file of cases in your area that have come to court in the last month. Use the Internet and local papers for your investigations. (ICT)
- Find out what you can about your own MP. What area do they cover? Which party do they stand for? What is an MEP? (E)

SAYING NO

PURPOSE: To bring over the point that to say no is sometimes the only way to stay in control of your own life and staying on the right side of the law.

TEACHER INFORMATION:

Staying in control is vital. Saying no is only one of several main choices.

There are ten safe choices....

1. Say no and mean it. Look the person in the eye.
2. Be a broken record. If you don't want to do something keep saying so over and over again.
3. Stay cool at all times. Never rise to the bait.
4. Think of all your positive qualities. Talk about your good points.
5. Change the subject. Talk or do something else.
6. Ignore those who are taunting you. They are not worth your attention.
7. Avoid the situation. Choose your friends carefully.
8. Stay in a safe group. Remember there is always safety in numbers.
9. Walk away and leave temptation.
10. Remember it is your free choice. You have the right to feel safe.

KEY ACTIVITY (E)
YOU WILL NEED:

Create a situation where a group have decided to commit a crime but one member of the group does not want to take part. Act out what takes place. Discuss with the rest of the class what takes place.

FURTHER IDEAS:

- How do you think minor crime could be reduced in your area? Make a plan showing where most crimes occur. (M)
- Write out a list of situations at school where someone might need to say no. (E)
- When is it important for adults to say no? (E)

THE LAW AND YOUNG PEOPLE

CAR CRIME

PURPOSE: To discuss the effects of car crime on the individual and the victim.

TEACHER INFORMATION:
It is important to stress how important a car may be to someone. It can often be their most expensive possession and they may have to use it for a variety of reasons e.g. medical emergency. Imagine what it would be like to suddenly find you were without your car.

If your family or friends have a car...
- Make sure that they have an immobiliser fitted.
- Make sure that nothing of value is left on display.
- Security mark the audio equipment.
- Always lock the car even when they are at home.

On average a car is broken into every 25 seconds.
A stolen car is 2,000 times more likely to be involved in an accident than a legally owned one.
Car crime costs Britain over £3 billion a year.
Less than 10% of all valuables stolen from cars are ever recovered.

REMEMBER:
- Joyriding is stupid and very dangerous not only for those taking the car but for everyone else. It is also an inconsiderate act.
- After their home a car is often a person's most valuable possession.
- What starts as a theft can lead to death
- Car thefts make up around a third of all crimes reported.
- One in four of all cars reported missing are never found.

KEY ACTIVITY (M)
YOU WILL NEED: paper, pencil.

Carry out a car crime survey in your area with the help of parents and local residents. Compile some graphs and charts so that you can show your findings.

FURTHER IDEAS:
- Perform an anti-car crime play and present it to staff, children and parents and then to perhaps the local secondary school. (E)
- Discuss the possibilities of setting up motor projects to help your friends learn more about machine safety and the danger of car crime. (DT)
- Produce a video on the dangers of joyriding. (DT)
- Design a car security badge and poster for distribution around the school (A).

THE LAW AND YOUNG PEOPLE

ALCOHOL, DRUGS, SOLVENT ABUSE AND THE LAW

PURPOSE: To explain the law relating to each of these issues.

TEACHER INFORMATION:

Alcohol and the law
- At 14 you can go into a bar with an adult but you cannot buy or drink alcohol.
- At 16 you can drink beer or cider in a pub but only with a meal.
- At 18 you may buy alcohol, but if you drive with excess in your blood you will lose your driving licence.
- All these are with the landlords permission only.
- In many towns and cities it is now illegal to walk around the streets drinking alcohol.

Drugs and the law
Supplying drugs does not have to involve large amounts. Penalties for supplying are more severe than personal possession. Looking after drugs for someone, or going and buying them are all offences.

Drugs are divided into three classes:
A. (Most dangerous) e.g. Cocaine, Heroin, Ecstasy, LSD.
B. Amphetamines and Barbiturates.
C. Herbal Cannabis, Cannabis Resin, Benzodiazepine, Tranquillisers and Anabolic Steroids.

By injecting some substances they can become Class A. Often class A and B drugs get mixed up.

Maximum penalties for drug offences

CLASS	POSSESSION	PRODUCTION	TRAFFICKING
A.	7 years	Life	Life
B.	5 years	Life	14 years
C.	2 years	5 years	5 years

All offences include unlimited fines.

Solvent abuse and the law
In 2002 solvent sniffing cost 63 young lives.

Some youngsters will sniff solvents instead of taking alcohol. The elements of danger are greater and they are cheap and easy to obtain. Addicts get hooked on the hallucinations which result from the habit. These can often be dangerous, unpleasant and frightening.

Sniffing can kill at the first attempt and it can affect the heart.

'Under the Intoxicating Substances Supply Act (1985) it is a offence to supply a person under 18 with a substance that the supplier believes will be used to achieve intoxication.'

KEY ACTIVITY (E)
YOU WILL NEED: paper, pencil.

Imagine that you have been witness to a glue sniffing session. Recount your experiences either in a poem, rap, a story or as a tragic newspaper report.

FURTHER IDEAS:
- Put together a song or a rap on the evils of drugs, alcohol and solvent abuse. (Ms)
- Get someone from social services or a help organisation to come in and talk about either drugs, alcohol or solvent abuse. (E)
- Draw a large poster on the dangers of alcohol. (A)

THE LAW AND YOUNG PEOPLE

TRESPASS AND VANDALISM

PURPOSE: To make youngsters more aware of the basic problems within their own area.

TEACHER INFORMATION:

Vandalism causes a lot of damage every year. It can take a number of forms such as breaking windows, damaging cars, phone boxes, fences and people's houses.

At least 1,000 telephone boxes are vandalised or attacked every week. Damage to these phones can cost lives.

Often schools, churches and public buildings e.g. unmanned railway stations are targeted.

If there are problems it is important that the area is cleaned up and the community take a pride in where they live. This often helps to decrease crime.

It is very important that children stay away from railway lines and the surrounding areas. The overhead cables carry 25,000 volts of electricity. Express trains can travel up to 140 mph and high speed trains take one and half miles to stop.

Trains cannot swerve like other vehicles to avoid obstructions or missiles as they run on tracks. Obstructing a railway line is a very serious criminal offence.

Sometimes graffiti can be a problem. This can reduce the value of properties, lower the tone and indicate that the people in the area don't care. It needs to be removed quickly.

Trespass is when someone enters another person's land unlawfully.

Motorways can also be very dangerous places and somewhere you should not trespass. With cars travelling at very high speeds there is little chance of someone walking along the carriageway surviving. You should also never throw objects at cars from the bridges.

Vandalism and trespass are very difficult to combat. If you have any information on these crimes please contact the police immediately.

KEY ACTIVITY (DT,M)

YOU WILL NEED: paper, pencil.

Conduct a survey looking at vandalism in your area. Ask yourself some of the following questions:
Can you see any abandoned cars?
Is there a lot of graffiti around?
Are local schools at risk?
Do the young people have anything to do?

FURTHER IDEAS:

- Write an anti-vandalism letter that could be sent to local households. (E)
- Organise an anti-vandalism poster competition. (A)
- Make a video about vandalism or trespass. (ICT)
- Investigate the cave paintings from thousands of years ago. (H,ICT)
- Ask the local police officer to come in and talk about the dangers of trespassing. (E)

THE LAW AND YOUNG PEOPLE

SHOPLIFTING AND OTHER FORMS OF THEFT

PURPOSE: To look at the seriousness of shoplifting.

TEACHER INFORMATION:
Theft and shop crime are major concerns for us all. Can you think of any ways of combating these problems in your area? There are a whole range of things that could be done to reduce the number of goods stolen from your locality.

If children know of someone who is stealing from a shop it is vital that they try and deter them. They may be afraid to confront them by themselves. If so then they should tell a parent, teacher or youth leader. They may be able to tackle the problem without telling the culprit who has brought the problem to their attention.

- Mobile phones and bikes are both at risk from theft.
- Mobile phones should be security marked and kept out of view.
- Bicycles should have their frame marked and have a code cycle sticker.
- You should take a photograph of your bike.
- Always lock it to something solid such as a lamp post.
- Use a solid metal lock rather than a chain.
- If possible take off the front wheel and lock it to the back wheel and frame.
- Make sure you know where your purse or wallet are.
- Keep keys somewhere safe.
- Keep valuables out of sight.
- Leave valuable jewellery at home.

KEY ACTIVITY (E)
YOU WILL NEED: paper, pencil.

Re-enact an interview between a suspected shoplifter and the security officer of a major department store. Now get the rest of the people in the class to decide whether or not they are telling the truth. Take a vote on it.

FURTHER IDEAS:
- Carry out some research into shoplifting in your area. (M)
- Produce and circulate a leaflet about crime prevention. (A,DT)
- Put on a short play explaining the wrongs of stealing. (E)
- Contact the local police and set up a cycle marking project. (DT)

THE LAW AND YOUNG PEOPLE

KEY LINKS

MATHEMATICS: Saying No
Car Crime
Shoplifting And Other Forms Of Theft

ENGLISH: What Is The Law?
Saying No
Car Crime
Alcohol
Drugs And Solvent Abuse
Vandalism And Trespass
Shoplifting And Other Forms Of Theft

SCIENCE:

HISTORY: What Is The Law?
Vandalism And Trespass

GEOGRAPHY:

DESIGN AND TECHNOLOGY: Car Crime
Vandalism And Trespass
Shoplifting And Other Forms Of Theft

MUSIC: Alcohol
Drugs And Solvent Abuse

ART & DESIGN: Car Crime
Alcohol
Drugs And Solvent Abuse

PE:

ICT: What Is The Law?
Vandalism And Trespass

RE:

THE LAW AND YOUNG PEOPLE

USEFUL CONTACTS

DRUGS

ADFAM
Confidential support and information for families and friends of drug users
Waterbridge House, 32-36 Loman Street,
London SE1 0EH
Tel: 0207 928 8898 (Mon-Fri 10am-5pm)
Website: www.adfam.org.uk

DRUG MISUSE INFORMATION SCOTLAND
1st Floor, Gyle Square, 1 South Gyle Crescent,
Edinburgh EH12 9EB
Tel: 0131 551 8753
Website: www.drugmisuse.isdscotland.org

DRUGSCOPE
32-36 Loman Street, London SE1 0EE
Tel: 0207 928 1211
Website: www.drugscope.org.uk

HEA DRUG CAMPAIGN (DCOS)
They will give you details of free allocations and cost effective purchase options
Tel: 01304 614 731 (England only)

HEALTH EDUCATION AUTHORITY
Trevelyan House, 30 Great Peter Street,
London SW1P 2HW
Tel: 0207 222 5300

HEALTH EDUCATION BOARD - SCOTLAND
Woodburn House, Canaan Lane,
Edinburgh EH10 4SG
Tel: 0131 536 5500
Website: www.hebs.scot.nhs.uk

NATIONAL DRUGS HELPLINE
offers free confidential advice about drugs
Call Frank: 0800 77 66 00 (freephone 24-hour)
Website: www.talktofrank.com

NETWORK VSA
Solvent Abuse Resource Group,
28 Penny Street, Blackburn, Lancashire. BB1 6HL
Tel: 01254 677 493
Website: www.airtime.co.uk/users/sarg

RELEASE
Confidential helpline offering advice on drug use and legal issues
388 Old Street, London EC1V 9LT
Tel: 08457 36 36 36 (24-hour)
Website: www.release.org.uk

RE-SOLV
Support and information relating to solvent and volatile substance abuse
Freephone: 0808 800 2345 (Mon-Fri 9am-5pm)
Website: www.re-solv.org

TACADE
Produce a range of support materials for use in and out of the classroom
Old Exchange Buildings, 6 St. Ann's Passage,
King Street, Manchester M2 6AD
Tel: 0161 836 6850
Website: www.tacade.com

THE SITE
Drug information for young people
Website: www.thesite.org.uk

THE CHILDREN'S LEGAL CENTRE
Tel: 01206 873 820
Website: www.childrenslegalcentre.com

USEFUL CONTACTS

SMOKING

ASH (Action on Smoking and Health)
102 Clifton Street, London EC2A 4HW
Tel: 0207 739 5902
Northern Ireland The Ulster Cancer Foundation, Block 24, Pavillion 2, Belvoir Park Hospital, Belfast BT8 8JR. Tel: 0289 049 2007
Scotland 8 Frederick Street, Edinburgh EH2 2HB
Tel: 0131 225 4725
Wales 220c Cowbridge Road East, Canton, Cardiff CF5 1GY. Tel: 0292 064 1101
Website: www.ash.org.uk

NATIONAL CHILDREN'S BUREAU
Solvent Misuse Project, Information Service
8 Wakley Street, London EC1V 7QE
Tel: 0207 843 6000
Website: www.ncb.org.uk

QUIT
National charity that helps people to stop smoking.
Ground Floor, 211 Old Street, London EC1V 9NR
Tel: 0800 00 22 00
Website: http://www.quit.org.uk

QUIT (Northern Ireland)
Tel: 01232 663439

ALCOHOL

AERC
The Alcohol Education and Research Council
Room 408, Horseferry House, Dean Ryle Street,
London, SW1P 2AW
Website: www.aerc.org.uk

ALANON FAMILY GROUPS UK AND ALATEEN
Al-Anon offers understanding and support for families and friends of problem drinkers. Alateen, a part of Al-Anon, is for young people aged 12-20 who have been affected by someone else's drinking, or young people with friends or family who are problem drinkers.
61 Great Dover Street, London, SE1 4YF
Tel: 0207 403 0888 (24-hour)
Northern Ireland Peace House, 224 Lisburn Road, Belfast BT9 6GE. Tel: 0289 068 2368
Scotland Mansfield Park Building, Unit 6, 22 Mansfield Street, Partick, Glasgow G11 5QP
Tel: 0141 339 8884
Website: www.al-anonuk.org.uk

ALCOHOLICS ANONYMOUS
Tel: 0845 769 7555
Website: www.alcoholics-anonymous.org.uk

ALCOHOL CONCERN
Offers general information about alcohol. Call to find your nearest alcohol advisory service.
Waterbridge House, 32-36 Loman Street,
London SE1 0EE
Tel: 0207 928 7377
Website: www.alcoholconcern.org.uk

DRINKLINE
Gives confidential information and advice and can put you in touch with your local alcohol advice centre for one-to-one help. Available in both English and Welsh
Tel: 0800 917 8282 (freephone,
Mon-Fri 9am-11pm, Sat-Sun 6pm-11pm)

HEALTH PROMOTION WALES
2nd Floor, Golate House, 101 St Mary Street,
Cardiff, CF10 1DX
Tel: 0292 026 1400
Website: www.hpw.org.uk

NARCONON PROGRAMME
Effective Solutions To Drug Addiction & Alcoholism
Tel: 0800 169 4803
Website: www.drugrehab.co.uk

USEFUL CONTACTS

AGE CONCERN
Chairty promoting the well-being of older people and positive attitudes towards ageing.
Tel: 0800 00 99 66 (helpline)
Website: www.ageconcern.org.uk

ANTI-BULLYING CAMPAIGN
Trained counsellors on hand to help with your problems.
Tel: 0207 378 1446

BARNARDOS
Chairty that works with vulnerable children and young people in the UK.
Tel: 0208 550 8822
Website: www.barnardos.org.uk

BRAKE
Road Safety Campaign
PO Box 548, Huddersfield HD1 2XZ
Tel: 01484 559 909
Website: www.brake.org.uk

CRIME CONCERN
Rail and Community Safety
Beaver House, 147-150 Victoria Road, Swindon, Wiltshire SN1 3UY
Tel: 01793 863 500
Website: www.crimeconcern.org.uk

CHILD ACCIDENT PREVENTION TRUST
4th Floor, Cloister Court,
22-26 Farringdon Lane, London EC1R 3AJ
Tel: 0207 608 3828
Website: www.capt.org.uk

CHILDLINE
Tel: 0800 1111 (freephone, 24-hour)
Website: www.childline.org.uk

DTI HOME SAFETY NETWORK
Tel: 01287 635 834
Website: www.dti.gov.uk/homesafetynetwork

ROYAL SOCIETY FOR THE PREVENTION OF ACCIDENTS - RoSPA
RoSPA House, Edgbaston Park,
353 Bristol Road, Birmingham B5 7ST
Tel: 0121 248 2000
Website: www.rospa.co.uk

THINK ROAD SAFETY
Website: www.thinkroadsafety.gov.uk

NSPCC
Child protection Helpline.
Tel: 0808 800 5000
Website: www.nspcc.org.uk
Website: www.there4me.com

ISPCC IRELAND
Protecting children's rights in Ireland
20 Molesworth Street, Dublin 2
Tel: 0167 94944
Website: www.ispcc.ie

SAMARITANS
Advice and counselling for the depressed and despairing.
Tel: 08457 90 90 90 (24 hour helpline)
Ireland Tel: 1850 60 90 90
Website: www.samaritans.org.uk